Our Debt to Greece and Rome

EDITORS

GEORGE DEPUE HADZSITS, PH.D.

DAVID MOORE ROBINSON, PH.D., LL.D.

CICERO
AND HIS INFLUENCE

BY

JOHN C. ROLFE, Ph.D.

COOPER SQUARE PUBLISHERS, INC.
NEW YORK
1963

Published 1963 by Cooper Square Publishers, Inc.
59 Fourth Avenue, New York 3, N.Y.
Library of Congress Catalog Card No. 63-10281

Printed in the United States of America
by Sentry Press, Inc., New York, N. Y. 10013

EDITORS' PREFACE

CICERO'S career, influence and meaning are most important in determining *Our Debt to Greece and Rome,* which the volumes of this series are aiming to make clear. Cicero, the great mediator, has enshrined the significance of ancient Rome in the hearts of many, and our debt to him is one of the spirit, of enlightenment and charity, of love of truth and liberty. So great is that debt that another volume in the Library is reserved for Cicero, the philosopher.

Professor Rolfe has written a defense of Cicero, such as will commend itself to twentieth century thought. That Cicero's star has, at times, suffered an eclipse is not astonishing. Ignorance may blot out even a gospel of light. But the appraisal of the future is apt to be more cordial than it has sometimes been in the past.

The story of the influence of Cicero is one to command admiration and wonder. Such movements as Christianity, the Renaissance

[v]

and the French Revolution drew direct inspiration from this Roman of long ago. The charm of his language and the reasonableness of his thought have contributed to Cicero's enduring influence. It was Cicero's persuasive eloquence that made the world pay heed to his message. Centuries after his death, Cicero has remained a living presence, real to members of the English Parliament, real to Thomas Jefferson, and for us he remains an immortal, who, above all, demonstrates the unity of civilization and the common aspirations of the race. It is reserved for only a few to belong to yesterday, to-day and to-morrow and to lead mankind by wisdom that possesses universal validity.

" Quid enim est aetas hominis, nisi ea memoria rerum veterum cum superiorum aetate contexitur? " This is the way to humanism.

CONTENTS

CONTENTS

CICERO
AND HIS INFLUENCE

CICERO AND HIS
INFLUENCE

I. SOME VERDICTS, ANCIENT
AND MODERN

ONE of the most dramatic incidents in all the records of the past is the following, which is related by Plutarch. The emperor Augustus, he tells us, came unexpectedly upon one of his grandsons and found him reading from a volume of Cicero. The boy was startled and tried to hide the book under his gown; but the emperor took it from him and, standing by his side, read for a long time in silence. Then he handed the book back with these words: "An eloquent and learned man, my child, and a true lover of his country."

It does not require unusual visualizing power to bring before the mind's eye the panorama that Augustus must have witnessed, as he listened to that voice from the past, and thought of all that had occurred since the hand that wrote the words was nailed to the rostra and the tongue that pronounced them was stabbed by Fulvia's vengeful bodkin.[1] Only the cinema could do the scene full justice, with a "close-up" of Augustus, his handsome face "registering" deep thought, followed by a series of wonderful pictures, beginning with Cicero's first recognition of the future ruler of the world as the boy whom he had seen in his dream let down from heaven on a golden chain and presented with a whip by Jupiter,[2] and ending with the brutal murder of a lonely and disappointed old man on the shore near Formiae.

Somewhat different is the verdict rendered by an editorial writer in a recent issue of the New York *Times*.[3] In the course of some remarks on letter-writing he says: "Was Cicero, that everlasting word-monger, letter-writer, and self-praiser, ever natural save in his megalomania and his whining?" Although this critic goes on to speak of Cicero's *Letters*, his estimate of the great Roman is that of the schoolboy (not the average schoolboy, let us hope) whose acquaintance with the orator is limited to the conventional "six orations" demanded for admission to college. In the

judgment of the American newspaper man
Cicero was a " word-monger," in that of the
Roman emperor and great reconstructionist he
was λόγιος, a word which, like not a few
Greek vocables, defies translation by a single
term; it means " a master of words," and may
be used either of a speaker or of a writer.

I have assumed that Plutarch's tale is
founded upon fact, and that Augustus used
either the Greek word or a Latin equivalent;
probably the former. Naturally, the literary
judgment of an American journalist is entitled
to more respect than that of a Roman emperor, as such; but Augustus was himself a
fastidious stylist, and his opinion on matters
of diction is not to be despised. " He cultivated a style of speaking," says his biog-
rapher,[4] " which was chaste and elegant,
avoiding the vanity of attempts at epigram
and an artificial order, and as he himself expressed it, ' the noisomeness of far-fetched
words,' making it his chief aim to express his
thought as clearly as possible. He looked upon
archaizers and innovators with equal con-
tempt, as faulty in opposite directions, and he
sometimes had a fling at them, in particular
his friend Maecenas, whose ' unguent-dripping

curls,' as he calls them, he loses no opportunity of belaboring and pokes fun at them by parody; and as for Mark Antony, he calls him a madman for writing rather to be admired than to be understood." Aulus Gellius, in his *Attic Nights,* refers to Augustus as a rival of the elegant style of his father, the great Julius.

Our modern critic goes on to say: " In all his letters to Atticus, for instance, however valuable they may be to students of Roman history or professed Ciceronians, there is mighty little for the modern reader, who seeks in the past something human, the ancient that is contemporary." Beside this opinion of the *Letters* we may set that of Mackail in his *Latin Literature:* " The art of letter-writing," says the English scholar, " suddenly arose in Cicero's hands to its full perfection. It fell to the lot of no later Roman to have at once such mastery over familiar style, and contemporary events of such engrossing and everchanging interest on which to exercise it. All the great letter-writers of more modern ages have more or less, consciously or unconsciously, followed the Ciceronian model. England of the eighteenth century was particularly

[6]

rich in them; but Horace Walpole, Cowper, Gray himself, would willingly have acknowledged Cicero as their master." Perhaps Mackail would be classed by the sage of the *Times* as a " professed Ciceronian," whatever that may be. That is hardly true, however, of Barrett Wendell, who in *The Traditions of European Literature* writes of Cicero: " His letters are those of an accomplished gentleman, in the finer sense of the word; they show his complete urbanity of social habit; they also show his politely alert familiarity with intelligent thought, with fine art and with literature, Greek and Latin. Here if ever in the whole course of literature you find yourself in thoroughly good company; and thoroughly good company implies highly trained minds and manners." Above all, the charge of undue partiality to the classics cannot be brought against Mr. H. G. Wells, who declares in his *Outline of History* that the orations and private letters which Cicero has left us make him one of the most real and living figures of the period to the modern reader.

These widely divergent opinions are typical, for no Roman, perhaps no historical personage, has been more extravagantly praised or more unjustly assailed and belittled than Cicero. The eulogies of Middleton and Trollope, of whom the former, in the words of Macaulay, " composed a lying legend in honor of St. Tully," and the slanders of Drumann and Mommsen, are equally unreasonable; but both the praise and the censure are testimony to Cicero's importance in his own day and to his position of influence in modern times. He was, as Ferrero says, in Roman history and in the history of that European civilization which began with Rome, the first statesman belonging to the intellectual class. Of the dynasty which he founded, of men of letters who were either the pillars of the state or workers of revolution, he possessed, in Ferrero's opinion, all their finer qualities and of their defects only the most venial. " Cicero," he says, " may have made many a grave political error, but none the less his historical importance can compare with that of Caesar and is but little inferior to that of St. Paul and St. Augustine." [5]

It cannot be denied that one of Cicero's most conspicuous failings was vanity, a vanity which he naïvely reveals in his private correspondence, which appears also in his orations and in his public utterances. This characteristic, however, deplorable as it is, has been exaggerated by unfriendly critics, when judged not only by ancient standards, but even by those of the present day. It is only fair to bear in mind that Cicero, as a "new man," [6] making his way against the opposition of a powerful clique, was forever on the defensive, that he felt the constant necessity of emphasizing his own merits and dwelling upon his services to his country. This charitable view was held among his own countrymen by Quintilian, who writes: [7] "Cicero has been subjected to no small amount of criticism in this regard, although in his speeches he boasted of his exploits more than of his eloquence. And even for that he had some justification, since he was either defending men who had helped him to put down the conspiracy or was replying to envious detractors. For the latter, however, he was no match, and since he suffered exile in return for saving his country, his frequent mention of what he did in his consulship may seem to have been self-defense quite as much as boastfulness." Another excuse for Cicero's self-praise is given by Gille Ménage, as quoted by Isaac

D'Israeli: [8] " Cicero," he says, " has boasted of the great actions he has done for his country, because there is no vanity in exulting in the performance of our duties; but he has not boasted that he was the most eloquent orator of his age, though he certainly was, because nothing is more disgusting than to exult in our intellectual powers." If this excuse is accepted as valid, Cicero stands justified: for although the modern reader finds even the frequent allusions to his services to his country distasteful, it is certainly true that he is modest in alluding to his oratorical powers. Thus he says at the beginning of the *Defense of Archias:* " If I possess any talent, gentlemen of the jury, and I know how slight it is, or any skill in speaking, to which I confess I have given no little attention, etc." Even in mentioning his services to his country he sometimes gives the credit to a higher power, not only in his orations, where he might be suspected of insincerity, but even in his private letters. Thus he writes to Atticus of " that condition of our country which you attribute to my sagacity, but I to divine wisdom."

This is very far from the " girlish vanity," with which he is charged by Macaulay.[9] To mention modern instances were invidious, but it would not be at all difficult to match Cicero's vanity by conspicuous examples in our own day, as well as among the orator's countrymen and contemporaries. Caesar's arrogant words and deeds, as catalogued by Suetonius, convict him of greater conceit than is shown by Cicero; but Caesar's vanity, which extended to his personal appearance, is overshadowed by his more picturesque qualities and is for the most part forgotten. The boastful and arrogant Julius of Shakespeare's tragedy is after all not unlike the Caesar of the period just before his downfall and death.

Modesty too, especially in modern times, does not always differ from vanity except for being in "better form." In the words of Francis Bacon in his essay *Of Vain Glory,* "excusations, cessions, modesty itself well governed, are but acts of ostentation." Furthermore, the line which divides vanity from proper self-respect cannot always be drawn with perfect accuracy. As Bacon says in the same essay: "Socrates, Aristotle, Galen were men full of ostentation. Certainly vain glory helpeth to perpetuate a man's memory; and virtue was never so beholden to human nature, as it received his due at the second hand. Neither had the fame of Cicero, Seneca, Plinius Secundus, borne her age so well, if it had not been joined with some vanity in themselves; like unto varnish, that makes seelings not only shine, but last." There can be no question, I think, that Cicero's vanity contributed in no small measure both to the success and to the merits of his career. He was always anxious to appear well in men's eyes, and he desired the good opinion, not only of his fellow citizens, but of posterity as well; although, as he writes to Atticus, he cared more for the approval of his conscience than for the opinions of all men. Anyone who is actuated by such feelings is certain to keep a watchful eye upon his conduct and to do his best to maintain high ethical standards. It was doubtless due in great part to his so-called vanity, the desire to appear well in the public eye, that, a man of no great physical courage, and somewhat inclined to be irresolute, he rose to the occasion and showed positive heroism in at least two great crises. It was this too, combined with his knowledge of history and his broad vision, which in a corrupt age made him a model provincial governor. The

lengths to which detractors of Cicero will go
is shown by Macaulay, who in the passage already referred to speaks of him as one " whose
whole soul was under the domination of a
girlish vanity and a craven fear." The latter
charge is as unjust as the former. Cicero did
not have that total absence and ignorance of
fear which all mortals admire, the valor which
blinds us to Caesar's defects; but for that
very reason he deserves the greater credit for
showing both moral and physical courage in
great emergencies. The man who defied Sulla,
impeached Verres, executed the Catilinarian
conspirators, joined Pompey's forlorn hope,
and despised Antony's swords was no craven.

It must be admitted that Cicero shows to
greater advantage in an emergency than at
other times, a course of conduct which corre-
sponds with his temperament. Cardinal
Newman, who thinks him irresolute and inconsistent, says on this point: " Nor can we
account for the firmness and resolution of his
consulate, unless we discriminate between the
case of resisting and exposing a faction, and
that of balancing contending interests."

Criticism is such a subjective matter, and
the views on every phase of Cicero's activity,

even his oratory, are so divergent, that it seemed to the writer better to give the opinions of a number of critics, rather than merely express his own view, which however will doubtless become apparent in the course of the essay. The number of opinions might be extended almost indefinitely, but we may content ourselves with the testimony of two more witnesses, an ancient and a modern, who give us the true standard by which to judge Cicero and other men who serve their country conscientiously. The elder Seneca, after expressing the wish that Cicero had been able to bear prosperity with more modesty and adversity with more firmness, continues: " But since no mortal man has achieved perfection, one should be judged according to the preponderance of one's merits or defects." Or as Burns puts it:

> " Then gently scan your brother man,
>   Still gentler sister woman;
> Though they may gang a kennin wrang,
>   To step aside is human."

As Leo points out,[10] when Cicero was studied as a man, in connection with all his many-sided activities, his merits far outweighed his defects; it was when an age of specialization examined him as a statesman, as a philosopher, as an advocate, or solely in the light of the revelations of his private letters, that his reputation suffered by comparison either with the leaders in statecraft and philosophy or with the perfect man. But a reaction has already begun and to-day Cicero is as a rule more justly judged than he has been at some times in the past.

II. CICERO'S POLITICAL IDEAL AND ITS INFLUENCE

THE Rome that Cicero loved was the old republic of the days of the Scipios; but as a recent writer has truly said,[11] he did not hope to see that condition of things restored. Contrary to the opinion of those who charge him with excessive conservatism, he realized that times had changed and that the old order could never exactly be renewed. He did, however, cling to the ideal of a free state, a republic in general like that of the old days, but adapted to changed conditions. Man has constantly been striving for freedom, but the dream of a government truly of the people, for the people and by the people has never been realized. It is doubtful whether it is possible of attainment, except in a small community in which all the citizens can take an active part in the administration of the state. Even there, men of exceptional ability and initiative are sure to assume control, for it is unfortunately not true that all men are born free and equal. To those who, like ourselves, live in a republic, the history of other republics, their successes and their failures, and the reasons for them, have a peculiar interest; and this is particularly true of the great Roman republic.

In Cicero's Rome the control of the government had fallen into the hands of a body of highly trained men, a ruling class theoretically fitted for duties of the most varied kind. The leading men of the Roman senate, the flower of her aristocracy, had filled the higher Roman magistracies, they were supposed to be able to take the field as commanders of armies equipped with the necessary military knowledge, and to govern provinces in various parts of the Roman world, which presented a great variety of administrative problems. In such a body there was place for men of prominence, constitutional leaders such as Scipio, but all were expected to be controlled by patriotism, precedent and inherited custom.

If the Roman senate had actually been a body of this kind, it is difficult to imagine a more efficient and satisfactory form of government, especially since the aristocratic ruling class was, at least nominally, chosen by the people. But in the first place, the unwieldy body of six hundred or more members, in the absence of a committee system, such as facilitates the transaction of business in our own Congress, was controlled by a small faction made up of ex-consuls. In Rome's earlier days the members of the senate, although men of high character as viewed through the mists of the past, often lacked the experience and broad training demanded by their complex duties; in particular, the lack of competent generals brought many disasters upon the state, which only indomitable courage and rugged endurance could survive. In later days, the efficiency of the senate was impaired by the corruption and indolence of some of its members and the restless and unscrupulous ambition of others.

Sallust, in his *Jugurthine War*, gives us a vivid picture of the condition of the nobility at the end of the second century before our era, when the Numidian prince gained victory after victory in the field or by the use of money, and could say almost truthfully of Rome: " A city for sale, and doomed to perish, if only it can find a purchaser! " [12] But amid the general corruption and incapacity, he has given us — in the person of Quintus

Metellus — the portrait of an ideal Roman
aristocrat. He was honest and incorruptible, a
trained soldier and skilful leader — admirable
in all respects, save for his haughtiness and
clannish devotion to his order. From other
sources we learn that he was an orator of no
mean ability and a writer of pure and elegant
Latin.

The statement that the members of the senate were chosen by the people also has to be
qualified. The senate was, it is true, made
up of ex-magistrates elected by popular vote,
and therefore might be said to be chosen by
the people. Juvenal, however, satirically
terms the people's right of suffrage the privilege of selling their votes;[13] and although he
adds that once upon a time they had bestowed
power and the command of legions, that was
before Cicero's day. Quintus Cicero, in his
Handbook of Electioneering,[14] thinks that a
few of the centuries into which the voters were
divided were willing to cast their votes without pay. Augustus, upon restoring the old-time
privilege of popular suffrage, found it necessary to enact penalties for bribery; and even
then in the two tribes to which he belonged
(by birth and by adoption) he had to resort to

the novel expedient of distributing a handsome sum to each elector, in order to prevent him from levying on any candidate.

The Roman republic was hampered, not only by the habit of buying and selling votes, and the prominence and advantage thus given to wealth, but also by that other bane of popular government, the political " boss." The malign influence of money began, as Lucretius tells us in his wonderful sketch of the origin of human society, with the discovery of the precious metals, which easily robbed the strong and the fair of their honors. Sallust, in the *Jugurthine War*, shows us in Gaius Marius an example of a new element in Roman politics, in the form of men whom the support of the commons and special emergencies raised to extraordinary and eventually to unconstitutional power. He was the first conspicuous and successful example of the type of man who eventually overthrew the old Roman republic, a type perhaps foreshadowed in Spurius Cassius and Spurius Maelius, although the evidence is too scanty to allow us to determine whether they were really seekers of absolute power or genuine benefactors of the people. Marius, Sulla and Caesar are specimens of the higher type of boss. There was also the lower type, who did not himself aspire to, or attain, the highest positions, but who controlled votes and was able to " deliver the goods." Horace says of men of this kind:

> Hic multum in Fabia valet, ille Velina;
> Cui libet hic fasces dabit, eripietque curule
> Cui volet importunus ebur.

Midway between these two were men like Clodius and Milo, who attained high office without rising to the highest grades, but who pushed the fortunes of other men or dragged down their enemies.

Still another disturbing factor, as in our own day, was " big business," represented by the *equites*, or knights, who had large sums of money invested abroad, the protection of which sometimes influenced the foreign policy of the republic.

Cicero has been criticized for transferring his allegiance from the popular party to that of the senatorial aristocracy. But it must be remembered that Cicero never was a democrat in the sense that he believed in the uncontrolled sovereignty of the people, any more than was Caesar, in spite of a more consist-

ently popular adherence. Both Cicero and
Caesar believed in a highly trained governing
class, which must of necessity be an aristocracy. Both men recognized the power of the
masses and courted their support, each in his
own way and in accordance with his ideals,
but neither was a genuine democrat. Caesar's
plans and ambitions advanced to a belief in a
one-man power, a thinly disguised monarchy.
Cicero hoped to have a prominent place in the
senate of his ideal commonwealth, but rather
as a wise councillor than as a military or political leader, a Laelius to a new Scipio; and for
the appearance of this Scipio he was ever on
the watch. For his own prospective position
he had trained himself from early youth, and
on his way to the consulship (which was an
essential preliminary to the position of influence to which he aspired) and after he had
attained it, his political principles were determined by the end which he had in view.
He was the opponent of all who aimed at
power by usurpation or unconstitutional
means, and devoted to those who promised to
be capable of restoring a government like that
of the old republic; he looked for a leader who
should be, not a virtual dictator or king, but

chief of the senate by virtue of rank and attainments. If we keep this general attitude of Cicero's in mind, we can the better understand his political career, which was not unduly inconsistent. Certainly it was much less so than that of many a prominent politician of to-day.

It is important also, in order to form a proper and fair estimate of his life-work, to get as clear an idea as possible of Cicero's personality; and fortunately the frank revelations of his correspondence enable us to do this with a great deal of certainty. As Ferrero has implied, he was an early representative of a type somewhat more familiar in our own day, the "scholar in politics." Such men are by training, and usually by inclination, fitted to govern wisely and well; but they are exposed to the suspicion of being theorists, and since they are no match for the practical politician, who is unhampered by inconvenient ideals, they often fail to achieve complete success. Cicero was primarily a student and a writer, but the only path by which he could arrive at the position to which he aspired was the "course of honors", formed by the higher Roman magistracies from the quaestorship to

the consulship. To be elected to these offices
he must gain friends and supporters, and having no taste for military life, which was then,
as it has often been in our own country, a sure
and easy way of winning the favor of his fellow citizens, he chose a forensic career.

To be eligible for appointment to the senate,
one must have held the office of quaestor; but
the fulfilment of that minimum requirement
did not give a commanding position. The
more influential among the senators had filled
one or more of the curule offices of aedile, praetor and consul, and the really powerful members of the body, both by virtue of their
experience and because their opinions on public questions were the first to be called for
by the presiding officer, were the ex-consuls
(*consulares*). These formed an inner circle
within the nobility, from which " new men "
were jealously excluded. A new man might
by his talents rise as high as the praetorship,
but the next step was ordinarily extremely
difficult. In Cicero's time conditions had not
greatly changed, at least so far as regular constitutional advancement was concerned, since
the days of Marius. Sallust tells us of the
consternation of Metellus, the consul com-

manding the army in Numidia, when Marius, who had reached the praetorship and was serving as lieutenant general under Metellus, asked for a furlough in order that he might go to Rome and stand for the consulship. After vainly trying to dissuade him from so audacious an act, Metellus grievously insulted Marius, and brought about his own eventual recall, by saying: " Don't be in a hurry to go to Rome; it will be soon enough for you to be a candidate when my son becomes one "; and at the time Metellus' son was a youth of twenty. Sallust adds: " The commons could bestow the other magistracies, but the nobles passed the consulship from hand to hand within their own order. No ' new man ' was so famous or so illustrious for his deeds, that he was not considered unworthy of that honor, and the office so to speak sullied by such an incumbency." [15]

To break into this charmed circle required either some special emergency or unusual good fortune. Special emergencies raised Marius seven times to the coveted honor; Cicero was aided by the fear which the nobles felt of Catiline and his designs, but also, as has been pointed out,[16] by good fortune. The first step was made easier by Sulla's increase of the number of quaestors to twenty and by the diminution in the number of available candidates caused by the sanguinary Social War. At the time of his election as aedile and praetor the popular party was in power, a situation which strongly favored the candidacy of a " new man." His only formidable competitors in the consular elections were Catiline and Gaius Antonius. The latter was a son of the great orator whom Cicero had attended in his early days, but a man of low character and heavily in debt, while Catiline had already been involved in an attempt at revolution. Caesar and Crassus were suspected of complicity in this so-called first conspiracy of Catiline, and it was feared that if Catiline and Antonius should be elected, the actual power would be in the hands of Caesar and his associate. Thus everything conspired to make Cicero's election easy.

Politics and the methods of politicians have not changed radically since the days of the Roman republic. We too have had our statesmen of high ideals and our " scholars in politics," and as a rule they have been hampered and prevented from carrying out their plans by the partisan and the practical politician. Whatever Cicero's mistakes and limitations may have been, it must be admitted by the fair-minded that his motives were lofty and pure and that he was a genuine patriot. His political ideal has perhaps been most nearly realized in Great Britain, with its highly educated ruling class and trained diplomatic corps, at least before the money power and modern Mariuses came to play a part in her councils. A study of Cicero's career might well lead us to demand a higher grade of preparation and training for political positions, so that we might have fewer ambassadors and consuls who date their first acquaintance with the language, history and customs of the countries to which they are assigned from the day of their appointment, and fewer legislators whose ideas of political economy are revealed by the provisions of the Fordney tariff-bill. Just what the influence of Cicero and his political ideals has actually been is traced more fully in Professor Abbott's book, appearing in this Series, but whenever government officials have been actuated by a high sense of responsibility and a genuine spirit of patriotism, they have consciously or unconsciously followed in the footsteps of Cicero.

III. HIS CAREER: A DEFENSE

MARCUS TULLIUS CICERO, son and grandson of a Marcus, was born on the third of January, 106 B.C., at Arpinum, a small hill-town at the foot of the Volscian mountains, about sixty miles southeast of Rome. There it is that the river Fibrinus joins the Liris, Horace's *taciturnus amnis*. His life covers the last days of the republic, one of the most important epochs in the history of Rome and of the history of the world. In the words of Rufus Choate:[17] " Next for instruction and impressiveness to the revolution by which a nation dies, is that in which, preserving its life, it is compelled to change a condition of freedom for the government of tyranny. And in this class the grandest, most bloody, memorable and instructive in the history of man, is that by which republican Rome became the Rome of the Caesars."

Although Cicero was not a native of the city of Rome, the men of Arpinum possessed the rights of Roman citizenship and were enrolled in one of the tribes (the *Cornelia*) into which the citizens were divided for political purposes. The family was one of some importance in its native place; Cicero's father was a man of education, who had attained equestrian rank. To this order, the great middle and commercial class, Cicero was consistently friendly, and he did his best to unite the nobles and the knights (*equites*) against the power of individual politicians. Although not a member of the nobility, and hence a " new man " in the political sense, Cicero was not, in the ordinary sense of the term a " self-made man." He was born to a good position, enjoyed a thorough education, and found his associates among the upper classes of citizens. He was not a man of the people, but his parallel today is to be found in the aristocratic statesmen of modern Italy. In his career we read the inner history of that senatorial " course of honors," the bare outline of which is proudly inscribed upon so many Roman monuments; and we learn a lesson of patient, conscientious endeavor and service, which is as valuable today as it was in the last pre-Christian century.

From his early youth Cicero was filled with a desire " far to excel and tower above the crowd," as he himself expresses it in one of his *Letters*. He was doubtless encouraged, if not originally inspired, by the success of his fellow-townsman Marius; but it is to his credit that he aspired to reach his goal by honorable means, not as Marius did, "at the sacrifice of loyalty and justice." Many young men dream dreams and have lofty ambitions; few are willing or able to make the sacrifices necessary for the realization of their hopes, or wise enough to resist the lure of "short cuts." Cicero's thorough preparation for his profession is in itself enough to make the study of his life valuable to the younger generations. His father sent him at an early age to Rome, and there he applied himself to his studies with such diligence as to become a pattern for his school-fellows. Following the usage of the day, he supplemented the instruction of the schools by attaching himself to the most celebrated orators of the day, Antonius and Crassus, attending them to and from the Forum, listening attentively to their public addresses, and enjoying the benefit of their private conversation. He was wise enough to realize, and here he may teach another valuable and needed lesson, that technical training

was not the only requisite for success, but that
an advocate must have broad general culture
and an abundant store of special knowledge in
various fields. He therefore gave some attention to philosophy, which at this time he studied rather as an aid to success in his profession
than for its own sake. He became an intimate
friend of the poet Archias, in whose defense
he later delivered one of his most famous orations, and from him he acquired a love of
good literature which exerted a profound influence upon his tastes and manner of life, as
well as upon his oratorical and literary style.
By association from the age of seventeen with
two of the most eminent jurists of that time,
both of whom bore the name of Quintus
Mucius Scaevola, he gained a thorough knowledge of the laws and political institutions of
his country. In this way he made himself one
of the greatest lawyers of antiquity, one who
not merely depended upon swaying the emo-
tions of a jury, but was able to take full advantage of the legal possibilities of a case.

A young noble commonly opened his forensic career by the impeachment of some prominent man. Cicero, on the contrary, began by
defending several citizens arraigned on various

charges, and throughout his life he usually appeared for the defense, rather than as prosecutor. In the most noteworthy of his early orations, the *Defense of Sextus Roscius of Ameria,* spoken in rebuttal of a charge of parricide brought by Sulla's influential freedman Chrysogonus, Cicero showed true courage and at the same time revealed his political tendencies; he also displayed the biting wit which helped him to win more than one case, but which, according to Plutarch, also made him many enemies. At this time Cicero and Caesar were in the same boat; for the latter was forced to flee from Rome because of his defiance of Sulla's command to divorce his wife Cornelia, the daughter of Marcus Cinna.

Cicero's early orations attracted attention and showed signs of promise, but he did not consider his training completed. Furthermore, his health had suffered from unremitting devotion to work, and the Social War, in the course of which he had himself served for a year under Pompeius Strabo, the father of Pompey the Great, had brought legal business almost to an end. He therefore resolved to go abroad and accordingly spent two years in study and travel in Greece and Asia Minor,

with a residence of some duration in Athens
and at Rhodes. At this time, and for many
years to come, there were two rival styles of
oratory at Rome, known respectively as the
Asianic and the Attic. Briefly, the aim of the
former was to impress and secure the attention of an audience either by fluency, by florid
and copious diction and imagery, or by epigrammatic conciseness. The Atticists, on the
other hand, took as their model the clearness
and simplicity of expression of which the great
Attic writers and speakers, Thucydides, Xenophon and Lysias were exemplars, avoiding excessive rhetorical embellishment and paying
little attention to rhythmical structure. The
rivalry of these schools of expression, which
extended also to literary style, may be traced
in the works of the great Roman writers.[18]
Each method had its merits, but each was
carried to an extreme by some of its followers.
The Attic style at its best is seen in Caesar's
Commentaries, which Cicero describes as
" naked in their simplicity, straightforward
yet graceful, stripped of all rhetorical adorn-
ment, as of a garment." Shakespeare, by
sheer force of genius, has grasped the essential
features of the two modes, and contrasted

them, in the speeches of Brutus and Mark Antony, in the tragedy of *Julius Caesar*.

The Asianic manner was followed by Cicero's great rival, Hortensius, and was the rule in the schools of Asia Minor. Cicero's natural inclinations were in the same direction; he had a tendency to copiousness which led Quintilian to say that nothing could be taken from Demosthenes, nothing added to Cicero. This tendency Cicero never entirely overcame; its excess was toned down by the instruction of Apollonius Molo of Rhodes, under whom Caesar also studied, and by Cicero's own good judgment, which enabled him to see the merits and failings of both styles and to steer a middle course.

It were tempting to follow Cicero's career in detail, but considerations of space make that impossible. At the age of thirty-one he was for the first time eligible for election to the quaestorship.[19] He at once became a candidate for the office, was duly elected, and was assigned to the province of Sicily, as his sphere of duty, under the ex-praetor Sextus Peducaeus, with headquarters at Lilybaeum. He was now in line for appointment to the senate, although not yet a member of the nobility. He teaches us another lesson by the energy and thoroughness with which he performed the duties of his office, particularly distinguishing himself by succeeding in sending supplies of grain to Rome at a time of great scarcity. He might well be pardoned for thinking that he had acquitted himself well; but his own estimate of the importance of his services and the impression which they made upon the general public may best be told in his own words: " On my way back from my province," he writes, " having stopped at Puteoli, a place where many fashionable folk gathered together, I was stunned when a man asked me when I had left Rome and what the news was there. When I answered that I was on my way home from my province, he said: ' Oh, by Jove! of course; from Africa, I believe.' Beginning to get angry and disgusted, I answered: ' No, from Sicily.' Whereupon another, with the air of one who knows everything, said: ' What! don't you know that our friend has been quaestor at Syracuse? ' "

The result of this experience was that Cicero never again voluntarily left Rome, except for brief periods of rest and recreation at his vari-

ous country seats. As he himself goes on to
say: "When I found, gentlemen of the jury,
that the Romans have dull ears but keen,
watchful eyes, I ceased to care what men
might think of me. I took pains to let them
see me with their own eyes every day." That
Cicero could tell this story and enjoy it shows
that, at that period of his life at least, he had
a sense of humor, in spite of his fixity of purpose; and no man with a sense of humor can
be utterly and hopelessly vain. The knowledge
of Sicily which he acquired, and the friend-
ships which he made, stood him in good stead
six years later, when he prosecuted Verres for
maladministration of the same province. It
was that impeachment which established him
in the position of "leader of the bar," which
had formerly been held by Verres' chief advocate, Quintus Hortensius, and it paved the
way for future political preferment.

Cicero was equally successful in his candidacy for the office of aedile, leading all his
competitors and attaining the position at the
earliest age allowed by law. He was now a
member of the nobility, with certain rights
and privileges which he enumerates as follows:
" a more important place for giving my vote

in the senate, the purple-bordered toga, the
curule chair, and the privilege of transmitting
my portrait to posterity." Cicero's implied
hope of a line of noble descendants was not
realized. Bacon says that great men have no
continuance, and Cicero had that claim to
greatness among others. We have no trace
of the family, which he raised to noble rank,
beyond the orator's son, Marcus. The younger
Cicero earned the praise of Brutus and his
whole army for his efficient military service,
Augustus made him consul and governor of
Syria, but he had the reputation of being over-
fond of wine. Pliny tells us that he got drunk
and threw a cup at Agrippa, and the author
of the *Natural History* adds the comment: " no
doubt this Cicero wanted to take from Mark
Antony, the murderer of his father, the palm
of drunkenness." [20] Of Cicero's conduct of the
aedileship we know little, but we may assume
that it was conscientious and efficient. Plutarch tells us that the Sicilians sent him gifts
of all kinds, which enabled him to reduce the
price of food, always a popular measure. In
his management of the public games and
shows, he aimed at a mean between extrava-
gance and stinginess; he did not spend more

money than he could afford, but his subsequent advancement indicates that he satisfied the people.[21]

His usual success attended Cicero's candidacy for the praetorship. The elections were twice postponed because of riots, and bribery was rampant, but the orator again led the field. He was given charge of the court dealing with cases of extortion, before which he had prosecuted Verres. There he brought about the condemnation of Licinius Macer, thus, as he naïvely writes to Atticus, gaining much more from the favor of the people than he would have gained from the support of Macer, had he been acquitted. It was in his praetorship that Cicero made his first political speech, advocating the passage of a bill of the tribune Manilius, which conferred upon Pompey supreme command and unlimited authority in waging war against Mithridates and Tigranes. This brilliant address of Cicero's, variously entitled *De Lege Manilia* and *De Imperio Cn. Pompei,* has sometimes been criticized and the speaker charged with insincerity. Pompey, however, was at this time at the height of his promise, if not of his fame, he had freed Rome from the menace of the pi-

rates, and Cicero might well think that he saw
in him the constitutional leader of the senate,
of whom he dreamed. The orator had an
opportunity too of furthering the interests of
the knights, whose business and property in
the provinces were threatened by the inroads
of Mithridates.

True to his principle of keeping in the public eye, Cicero declined appointment to a
province at the close of his term of office, and
devoted all his energies to his canvass for the
crowning honor of the consulship. In that de-
partment of politics he was not without skill.
As a matter of course he had a page (*nomenclator*), whose duty it was to keep him in-
formed of the names of the electors and
prompt him in case of forgetfulness; but he
ordinarily dispensed with the services of that
functionary, making himself personally familiar with the names of all prominent and influential citizens, as well as learning sundry
particulars about them. As Plutarch says:
" Whatever road in Italy Cicero traveled, it
was easy for him to name and point out the
estates and villas of his friends." But lest his
official duties should keep him from thoroughly
mastering the art of vote-getting, his brother

Quintus thoughtfully provided him with the *Handbook of Electioneering* to which reference has already been made; and this the candidate doubtless found helpful.

That Cicero's ambition to some extent regulated his conduct as an advocate, although doubtless censurable, is hardly to be wondered at, when one considers the nature of the prize and the difficulty which a "new man" had in winning it. It is well known that the conduct even of some of our better presidents is so affected by their desire for a second term, that the advisability has been more than once suggested of substituting for two possible terms of four years each, a single term of six years; and numerous other examples of the same kind might readily be given. Cicero can hardly be justified for thinking of defending his competitor Catiline against a charge of maladministration of the province of Africa; still less for the admission made to his friend Atticus, that he had the jurors whom he wished and " the greatest good-will on the part of the prosecutor." But he was not obliged to strain his conscience by defending the conspirator; as has already been said, he owed his election to the fear of Catiline's revolutionary designs, which gave him the reluctant support of the nobles.

Up to the year 54 B.C., as Cicero informs us, some eight hundred men had attained the consulship, but out of that number barely one-tenth had won renown in that high office. Fortune continued to favor Cicero by giving him the opportunity to make his administration in 63 B.C. memorable. In dealing with the conspiracy of Catiline, which came to a head after his election, the orator showed both sagacity and courage. He succeeded in establishing the guilt of the conspirators beyond the possibility of a doubt, and the *senatus consultum ultimum* [22] gave him justification, if not a strictly legal right, for putting Lentulus and his associates to death.

Another event of great importance which characterized his consulship, although less spectacular than the great conspiracy, was the proposal by the tribunes of an agrarian law, which for the first time since the Social War contemplated a distribution of grain to the commons. Such a proposal appealed to the commons and to oppose it called for moral courage of a high order. But the distribution of land to the veteran soldiers, for example those of Sulla, had not resulted favorably, and it was from that class that Catiline had drawn much of his support. Furthermore, the real purpose of the bill seems to have been the appointment of a commission of ten men for a term of five years with very extensive powers, apparently a potential political machine devised to oppose Pompey's growing influence. Cicero delivered four orations against this bill and secured its defeat, along with that of several other measures which threatened the credit or the safety of the state. Perhaps his most difficult task was in opposing a proposition to restore to full citizenship the sons of the men whom Sulla had proscribed, an action which was just in itself but fraught with perilous consequences because of the close connection of Sulla's constitution with the stability of the constitution and the consequent welfare of the state. The speech which he delivered against the proposition unfortunately has not come down to us, but it must have been a masterly effort; in connection with it Quintilian calls Cicero " that artist in swaying men's minds " (*ille tractandorum animorum artifex*).

After such a consulship, marked by so many triumphs of oratory and statesmanship, Cicero

looked forward to spending the rest of his life
in dignified leisure, a man of influence among
his senatorial colleagues because of his ability
and his rank. Up to that time fortune had
favored him, but the rest of his life was a
series of disappointments. His subsequent literary work, to which perhaps he owes his
greatest fame, was pursued as a means of consolation in times of disappointment and
trouble; this is indicated by the dates of these
works and is made clear by his own words in
certain of his *Letters*. Writing to his brother
Quintus, he says: "I am disappointed, my
dearest brother, that this time of my life,
which ought to be attended by a position of
authority in the senate, is either annoyed by
forensic labors or spent in literary work."
And in a letter to Marcus Marius he writes of
his court duties: "Not only did I find them
irksome formerly, when youth and ambition
spurred me on, and when besides I could refuse
to defend anyone to whom I objected, but under present conditions life is not worth living."

Cicero's enemies began their attacks at the
close of his consulship, when the tribune Metellus Nepos prevented him from making the
usual parting address to the people Shortly

afterwards Cicero incurred the deadly hatred
of that " stormy petrel of politics " Publius
Clodius Pulcher, who was afterwards untiring
in his efforts to bring about the orator's downfall.   Cicero might have saved himself by
accepting the invitation to join with Caesar,
Pompey and Crassus and make a quattuor-
virate out of the first triumvirate of 60 B.C.
Such a step would not only have secured his
safety, but it would have given him the position of influence to which he aspired. A practical politician would have embraced the
opportunity; that Cicero did not do so is strong
evidence of his sincerity, as well as of his courage. Pompey for a time held Clodius in check,
but finally consented to his adoption into a
plebeian family. Being thus made eligible for
the office of tribune of the commons, Clodius
brought about Cicero's banishment, on the
charge of having put a Roman citizen to death
without a trial. The orator's house on the Pala-
tine hill was thereupon pillaged and burned,
the ground on which it had stood was con-
secrated to Liberty, and his villas at Tusculum
and Formiae were destroyed. His banishment,
however, lasted only from April of the year
58 B.C. until August of the following year. His

recall was due in part to a falling out of Pompey and Clodius, but particularly to the superior strength of the lawless bands of Sestius and Milo, as compared with those of his arch-enemy, Clodius.

Cicero's return from exile was one of the great triumphs of his life. As he tells us in a long letter to Atticus, the bill for his recall was passed with flattering unanimity and enthusiasm on the part of all classes of citizens, and an unusual number of voters from outside of the city hastened to Rome to cast their ballots. On the journey from Brundisium, which occupied nearly a month, he was met everywhere by delegations offering their congratulations. When he arrived at the city, in addition to the large number whom he could call by name, there was no one, he tells us, that was known to his *nomenclator* that did not come to meet him, with the exception of such of his enemies as were unable to disguise or deny their enmity. The steps of the temples were crowded with people, the Forum and the Capitol were thronged, and all along his route he was greeted with applause.

The constant attacks of Clodius, which continued after Cicero's recall, and the growing friendship between Caesar and Pompey changed Cicero's attitude towards the triumvirate first to toleration and then to active support. It is at this period that we have a curious revelation of his vanity and his desire to appear well in the eyes of posterity, as well as in the opinion of his contemporaries. In a letter to Lucceius the orator begs him to write a history of the famous consulship, not adhering too closely to historical accuracy, but glorifying the consul as much as possible. He suggests that Lucceius should not include this work in the general history of Rome on which he was engaged, but should make it the subject of a special monograph. He believes that his consulate offers abundant material for such a work, and that it would arouse both the interest and the sympathy of his readers. Montaigne in his *Essays* dwells upon the thought that ambitious spirits, such as Cicero, solicit the historians of their time not to forget them, and Fortune, as if in spite, has preserved the vanity of the requests but destroyed the histories. There is no evidence, however, that the monograph was ever written.

The year 53 was marked by the death of Marcus Crassus in Parthia and the loss of the standards which Augustus was so proud of recovering. With Crassus died his son Publius, who had won distinction as one of Caesar's lieutenants in Gaul. The younger Crassus had been a member of the college of augurs, and Cicero was nominated for the vacant position by Pompey and Hortensius, and duly chosen a member of the ancient priesthood. Although this honor had no political significance, Cicero valued it highly because of the distinguished men who had enjoyed it in the past. It doubtless led him to study the history and traditions of the priesthood, on which he wrote a work which has not come down to us.

When Cicero was elected consul, in 63 B.C., the rich province of Macedonia had fallen to his lot,[23] but he turned it over to his colleague Antonius, as the price of his support against Catiline. He declined to take another in its place, having no desire to leave Rome for any purpose, least of all to enrich himself as a provincial governor. But in the year 51 B.C. a new law was passed, which provided that five years must elapse between the holding of a praetorship or a consulship and the rule of a province. This law, which may have been directed in part against Caesar, made it necessary to call upon the services of all available ex-magistrates; in consequence Cicero, much against his will, became governor of Cilicia. Not only was he reluctant to leave Rome, but on the way to his province and constantly during his term of office he urges his friends to see to it that his incumbency should not be for longer than a year. Civil war was already looming on the horizon; Cicero was anxious not to lose touch with the political situation at Rome, and there were besides private reasons which added to his unwillingness to be so far from home; but there was no help for it. It is characteristic of the " scholar in politics " that in preparation for his rule of the province he " wore out " his copy of the *Cyropaedia* of Xenophon by constant reading. If one is inclined to smile, or to sneer, at this academic performance, the success of Cicero's administration suggests that careful preparation for such a task is not after all a bad idea.

In his unwelcome office Cicero conducted himself in all respects admirably. He was scrupulously honest in his administration, although he was then, as at many other times, greatly in need of funds; he accepted no gratuities or favors; and he even refrained from profiting by means which were generally regarded as legitimate and proper. He did not have the trouble from the Parthians which he had feared, but he gained military victories over some of the mountain tribes which had revolted, and was hailed by his troops as *imperator*.[24] The senate honored his victory with a decree of thanksgiving and Cicero aspired to the still higher honor of a triumph. He wrote a long and detailed account of his administration to Cato, in the hope of enlisting his support. Cato, however, replied adversely, in spite of the fact that he had voted for a thanksgiving for Bibulus on account of much less important successes. But Bibulus was an aristocrat and Cato's son-in-law, and even Cato was not wholly and consistently incorruptible. It is characteristic of the orator's vanity, and of a growing loss of his sense of humor, that he continued to use the title *imperator,* even in letters to Caesar, and was attended by lictors with laurel-wreathed fasces, an entourage that was at times embarrassing, if not ridiculous.

On his return to Rome Cicero found cause for unhappiness in a realization of Pompey's incapacity and in knowledge of the growth of

Caesar's power, of which he had already had warning in letters from Rome, received during his absence. He was also seriously estranged from his wife Terentia, whom he finally divorced after thirty years of wedded life. The reason for this is not altogether clear; Terentia seems to have mismanaged his business affairs during his absence, and she is said to have had an imperious nature and a violent temper. As a matter of fact, Cicero was essentially a man's man. His view of women seems to have been similar to that of Metellus Numidicus, who, in his address to the people *On Marriage,* spoken during his censorship, delivered himself of the following sentiment: Si sine uxore vivere possemus, Quirites, omni ea molestia careremus; set quoniam ita natura tradidit, ut nec cum illis satis commode, nec sine illis ullo modo vivi possit, saluti perpetuae potius quam brevi voluptati consulendum est. Unlike the greater number of his famous contemporaries, Cicero was not strongly attracted by the fair sex. In one of his letters, writing of a dinner at which the notorious Cytheris was present, he says: Me vero nihil istorum ne iuvenem quidem movit umquam, ne nunc senem. No breath of scandal attaches to his

name until late times, and then the charges
against his fair fame are too extravagant and
too absurd to be taken seriously. A second
marriage, with his rich ward Publilia, was ob-
viously prompted by need of money, for which
he blames Terentia. It was not a successful
venture (*improbe Neptunum accusat, qui
iterum naufragium facit*), for Publilia's jealousy of Cicero's beloved daughter Tullia, and
her indifference, to say the least, at her death,
led to a speedy and final separation. Tyrrell
regards Cicero's strong affection for his
daughter, and his comparative indifference to
Terentia, as a Gallic trait, comparing the love
of Madame de Sévigné for "the prettiest girl
in France." He puts in the same class the
orator's strong attachment to the city of Rome,
as shown especially by his reluctance to leave
it at any time, and the orator's delegation of
religion to his wife as her particular province.[25]

Politically, the period was one of perplexity
and hesitation for Cicero. He was hostile to
Caesar's evident designs, but he feared his
power and rightly distrusted Pompey's ability
to cope with so formidable an antagonist. The
difference between the two men is exactly and
beautifully expressed (after the event, it is

true) by Lucan. Speaking first of Pompey, the brilliant poet of Nero's time says: [26]

" Nor came the rivals equal to the field;
  One to increasing years began to yield,
  Old age came creeping in the peaceful gown,
  And civil functions weigh'd the soldier down;
  Disus'd to arms, he turn'd him to the laws,
  And pleas'd himself with popular applause,
  With gifts and liberal bounty sought for fame,
  And lov'd to hear the vulgar shout his name.

＊　　＊　　＊　　＊　　＊　　＊　　＊

  Careless of future ills that might betide,
  No aid he sought to prop his falling side,
  But on his former fortune much rely'd.
  Still seem'd he to possess, and fill his place,
  But stood the shadow of what once he was."

He then compares Pompey to an old and sacred oak, wreathed with trophies of bygone wars, leafless and doomed to fall beneath the first gale, but still an object of veneration. Turning then to Caesar:

" But Caesar's greatness, and his strength, was
      more
  Than past renown and antiquated power;
  'Twas not the fame of what he once had been,
  Or tales in old records and annals seen,

But 'twas a valour, restless, unconfined,
Which no success could sate, nor limits bind;
'Twas shame, a soldier's shame untaught to
yield,
That blush'd for nothing but an ill-fought field.

  ** * * * * * **

Urging advantage, he improv'd all odds,
And made the most of fortune and of gods;
Pleas'd to o'erturn whate'er witheld his prize,
And saw the ruin with rejoicing eyes."

Caesar is then aptly compared with a thunderbolt.

That Cicero was still a dominant figure at this time is shown by Caesar's evident desire to secure the orator's neutrality, if not his active support. That he nevertheless remained firm, and finally decided, to join Pompey, is strong testimony to his devotion to his principles, as well as to his moral courage. Cicero has been blamed by many for lack of vision, in not realizing that the republic could not be saved and in not accepting the failure of liberty. On that point the words of Rufus Choate are pertinent: " Because now we are able to see that the struggle for liberty against mailed despotism, — of the senate and people of Rome against the spirit of Caesar in arms, say rather the spirit of the age, was unavailing, — shall we pronounce in our closets, that a patriot-senator, a man, made consul from the people according to the constitution, bred in the traditions, bathed in the spirit, proud of that high, Roman fashion of freedom, was a child not to have foreseen it as well? "

Cicero was prevented by illness from taking part in the battle at Pharsalus. After the defeat of his party he was pardoned by Caesar, who allowed him to return to Rome. There he devoted himself to literary work, producing the greater part of his philosophical treatises during the brief period which preceded Caesar's death. He occasionally emerged from his retirement — for instance, to ask for the pardon of Marcellus and Ligarius, in both cases successfully. The speech *For Marcellus* is a eulogy of Caesar's clemency, because of which the orator has sometimes been accused of insincerity. But Cicero may have had some faint hope that Caesar might after all turn out to be the long-sought leader, and that he would restore a constitutional government. Cicero's return to Rome was saddened by the knowledge that his brother and his nephew were making their peace with Caesar by throwing the blame for their disaffection upon the orator. Caesar's magnanimity under such trying conditions is strong testimony to the real fineness of his character.

Cicero took no part in the conspiracy against Caesar's life, although many of the assassins were his personal friends, but his public and private utterances must have given encouragement to the plotters. He hailed the result with joy, espoused the cause of the liberators, whom he believed to be the restorers of the republic, and plunged again into political life. But he was again disillusioned by the weakness of the leaders, and their inability to cope with the difficulties of the situation. Caesar's popularity with the commons had been so great, and Antony was so adroit a politician, that the expected results did not follow the assassination. Cicero nevertheless made a good fight, assailing Antony in the fourteen orations which are known as *Philippics* from a certain likeness to those delivered by Demosthenes against Philip of Macedon. When the so-called second triumvirate was formed in 43 B.C., Cicero's life was demanded by Antony, who succeeded in overruling Octavian's objections and placing the orator's name on the list of the proscribed. After making an attempt to escape by sea, Cicero was forced by bad weather and seasickness to return to land, where he was slain near his villa at Formiae. His life is briefly summed up by Ferrero as follows: "He had finished his work and had secured the claim to be regarded with Caesar as the greatest figure in this great epoch of Roman history."

IV. HIS CHARACTER

SOME features of Cicero's character, about which there has been the widest difference of opinion both in antiquity and in modern times, have already been briefly touched upon in other connections. In passing judgment upon his statesmanship, we must bear in mind that political parties, or factions, in Rome were based upon the interests of the classes — nobles, knights and commons — and not upon great national issues. Great problems there were, such as the agrarian question and the cost of living, the extension of citizenship — an issue which led to the devastating Social War — the establishment of harmony between the two great orders, and the selection of the list of jurors, which was for a long time a bone of contention between knights and nobles.[27] But none of these issues was the peculiar property of any political party or had its constant support. If we bear this in mind, Cicero's political principles seem as consistent as was to be expected or desired in such a time of uncertainty and disorder. Life is growth and change, and consistency is not invariably a jewel. Even the fear of the " deadly parallel column " is not always sufficient to hold the modern statesman in line, and the vacillation with which Cicero has been charged by some was, as has often enough been pointed out, largely due to shifts in the course of Roman politics and to the condition of the state. He was at first, as we have seen, the champion of the knights (his own order) and of the people against the tyranny of Sulla and the aristocracy. When he himself became a member of the senatorial order, his allegiance was naturally divided; but he still labored earnestly for harmony between the two orders, sometimes supporting the claims of the knights even when he thought them in the wrong. He always had the interests of Rome at heart; as Sir Philip Sidney expresses it: " Tully taketh much paynes, and many times not without poeticall helpes, to make us knowe the force love of country hath in us."

If Cicero's record as a statesman is on the whole the least successful part of his career, it is because he was too much of an idealist and not enough of a practical politician. In these respects he stood midway between Caesar and Cato. He lacked the adroitness and unscrupulousness of the former, but unlike the latter he sometimes compromised or made concessions to circumstances. If in his quest of the consulship he now and then sacrificed principle to policy, he was enabled in that office to render conspicuous services to his country, if not to save it from anarchy and devastation. Cato, on the other hand, was defeated in his candidacy for the praetorship, and his stiff-necked attitude prevented him from accomplishing as much good as he might otherwise have done. It is unfortunately true that the uncompromising reformer, who disdains to play the game of politics and to be content with relative rather than absolute improvement of conditions, seldom, if ever, accomplishes great things.

In his political life Cicero was confronted by four great crises: the conspiracy, his banishment, the civil war and his contest with Antony. In all except his exile he rose to the occasion, made his decision on the basis of what he believed to be his country's interests, and showed courage and efficiency. In banishment, which was a more personal matter, he does not appear in so favorable a light; but while one cannot but deplore his lack of fortitude, it is fair to remember that to the Romans in general separation from Rome was a greater calamity than we in our cosmopolitan age can readily realize, and with Cicero this attachment to the capital was even greater than that of the average Roman. Furthermore, Cicero was of a sensitive nature, keenly desirous of the good opinion of his fellow citizens and jealous of his influence in the councils of the nation. The very vanity that made him show courage at critical moments, and strive to be an ideal provincial governor, made the blow fall with greater weight. His expressions of regret at not having taken his own life seem to a modern reader cowardly and unworthy of a philosopher; but the feeling of the Romans about suicide differed radically from our own. Cato, a stock example of *constantia* in the schools of rhetoric, gained a surname and immortal fame by taking his own life at Utica, rather than survive the fall of the republic.

At a time when great fortunes were made by extortion in the provinces, and by other forms of profiteering, Cicero's integrity was

never called in question. He was at no time a
wealthy man, and he seems to have observed
the letter of the Cincian law, which forbade
the taking of fees by advocates. His tastes,
it is true, were somewhat luxurious and extravagant, although in a refined way, and after
he became a senator the social ambitions of
one not to the manor born led him into still
greater expense. He owned an hereditary es-
tate at Arpinum, as well as several country
and seaside villas in the neighborhood of
Rome and in Campania, besides lodges (*de-
versoria*) at Tarracina, Sinuessa, Cales and
Anagnia. The villas and lodges were a great
convenience, if not a necessity, for a public
character, because of the poor quality of the
inns in the country districts and smaller towns
of Italy. He was fond of books and works of
art, and he was a generous entertainer. As
to his resources, he tells us that he received
over a million dollars in the form of legacies,
but this is regarded by Tyrrell as rhetorical
exaggeration. Yet inasmuch as indirect payment for legal services was sometimes made
in that way, while obscure millionaires not
infrequently advertised themselves by legacies
to prominent men, the sum does not seem an

incredibly large one, compared for example with that which Augustus said that he had received from similar sources.[28] In any event, Cicero was often financially embarrassed, and his debts sometimes forced him to act contrary to his inclinations, for example in defending his former colleague Antonius against his own conviction as to what was right. Yet he seems always to have met his obligations in due time, although he was sometimes slow in making payment. He shows praiseworthy eagerness to discharge a debt of $35,000 to Caesar, at a time when he could not agree with Caesar's political course. We are told that Caesar, after his conquest of Gaul, had an abundance of gold, which he loaned either without interest or at a low rate, and thus put many of the senators under obligations, a piece of strategy which has a modern aspect. Doubtless Cicero was one of these, but he took pains to pay off the debt in order to have a free hand. It is equally to his credit, when one considers his financial difficulties, that he did not enrich himself at the expense of his province. His legitimate profits as governor nevertheless amounted to nearly $100,000, which he deposited with a banker in Ephesus.

This sum was taken by Pompey at the out-
break of the civil war with Caesar, so Cicero
tells us; but Tyrrell thinks he merely said so
to console his friend Rufus for the losses
which the latter had suffered. This, however,
seems to be purely a matter of opinion, un-
supported by evidence of any kind.

All in all, Cicero was, as has been said more
than once, a human, not an heroic personality.
He was warm-hearted and emotional, a good
friend but also a good hater and inclined even
to be vindictive. He lacked the forgiving
spirit of Caesar, which however was perhaps
prompted at times by motives of policy as
much as by clemency. He was quick to re-
ceive impressions and inclined to believe what
he himself wished to be true. His life, like
that of Horace, is particularly inspiring because all his defects were natural, all his merits
the result of education and efforts at self-
improvement.

We may conclude this chapter with the
opinions of two great Romans. Titus Livius,
the historian Livy, says of him: "If one
weighs his faults against his merits, he was a
great man, of high spirit, worthy of remem-
brance; to sound his praises would require a

Cicero for his eulogist." At a later time Quintilian writes: " I cannot see where Marcus Tullius anywhere failed to show the feeling of a good citizen. In proof of this we have his consulship, filled nobly, his upright management of his province and refusal of the vigintivirate,[29] and in the Civil Wars, which arose when he was an old man, a spirit which neither hope nor fear could prevent from uniting with the best side, that of the republic." Only the most rabid and unreasoning hatred and prejudice could take exception to these statements; no man of his day could show so clean a record, and few statesmen of any age would appear to better advantage, if their acts and thoughts were exposed to the same publicity as those of Cicero.

V. HIS POSITION AND INFLU-
ENCE AS AN ORATOR

THE synonym which is most frequently used, to avoid too frequent repetition of the name Cicero, is the word " orator." Many even of his detractors admit his eminence as a speaker. Quintilian declares that he was a perfect orator — a title which Cicero himself expressly disclaims — and that his name was synonymous with eloquence. Oratory was, in fact, the mainspring of his career and his efforts to perfect himself as a speaker were thorough and unremitting. He made a careful study of rhetoric, a subject on which he wrote a number of epoch-making works, he made himself familiar with the laws and customs of his country, and he buttressed these practical subjects with broad and deep culture. In the great triad of the *De Oratore*, the *Brutus* and the *Orator*, which forms a complete *corpus*, he has given us a discourse on the training of the orator, examples of great speakers among the Greeks and Romans with a criticism of their work, and a sketch of the ideal orator. His ideal makes clear the difference — which is as great to-day as it was in the past — between eloquence and mere elocution, between oratory and declamation. He believes that the orator must have a firm foundation of general knowledge and he points out the hollowness of choice diction and elegant language without sense. The perfect orator should be able to speak wisely and eloquently on any subject, with a dignified bearing and gestures. Of himself he says, in a passage which, like not a few of his utterances, is modest in its tone, that he owes his position as an orator, if he may lay claim to that title, to the schools of philosophy rather than to the teachers of rhetoric. In the *Defense of Archias* he praises literature in memorable words, not merely as an elegant recreation, but as contributing materially to the success of the pleader.

Cicero took oratory seriously, as he did all his work. His efforts to perfect himself in composition and in delivery were unremitting. Suetonius tells us that he continued to declaim in Greek, as well as in Latin, up to the time of his praetorship, and in Latin even when he was getting on in years. His anxiety to make a success of a plea was so great that, as he tells us himself, he very often arose to speak pale and trembling; and once in his early days he was so patently nervous that the presiding officer postponed the hearing of the case on which the young orator was to speak. To a thorough knowledge of the technique of public speaking he added an effective delivery, and in his rhetorical works he dwells greatly on the importance of action (*actio*). His delivery, as well as his composition, he perfected by painstaking effort and in spite of some natural handicaps. Plutarch tells us that his voice was at first full and strong, but harsh and unmodulated, and that it was forced by his vehemence into the higher notes. In another passage the same writer says that Cicero's utterance was at first weak, but that he improved it by a study of the famous actors Roscius and Aesopus. The comment of Seneca, the philosopher, is not easy to reconcile with that of Plutarch, for he compared Cicero's manner to the gait of an ambling or slow-stepping horse (*gradarius*). If both writers are to be trusted, the references may be to different periods of the orator's life, or Seneca may be contrasting his delivery with that of the vehement declaimers of his own day.

There were famous orators before Cicero: Cato the Censor, Tiberius and Gaius Gracchus, Antonius and Crassus, Hortensius. Of all these Cicero came into direct competition only with Hortensius, and then his victory was complete and decisive. It is probably true that Hortensius had seen his best days as a speaker by the time of the trial of Verres; it is not unlikely too that he depended on brilliance rather than on hard work and that it was in great part Cicero's legal acumen and his careful preparation which gave him the victory. Cicero's own early speeches fell far short of those of his later life, and it has been said that some estimate of the general level of the earlier oratory may be formed from Cicero's first efforts. Of these Tacitus says: "they are not free from the old-fashioned blemishes. He is tedious in his introductions, long-winded in his narrative parts, and wearisome in his digressions. He is slow to rouse himself and seldom warms to his work; only here and there do you find a sentence that has a rhythmical cadence and a flash-point at the finish." But both Quintilian and Tacitus declare that Cicero eventually revolutionized the art of Oratory both in style and in manner. The latter says: " Cicero was the first to give the proper finish to oratorical style. He was the first to adopt a method of selection in the use of words, and to cultivate an artistic arrangement; further he tried his hand at some flowery passages and was the author of some pointed sayings, at any rate in the speeches which he wrote when well on in years and towards the close of his career, that is to say, when his powers were well developed, and he had learned by experience and practice the qualities of the best type of oratory." Barrett Wendell, in his *Traditions of European Literature,* writes of Cicero's oratory: " His orations, whether legal or political, could have been produced by nothing less than assiduous and life-long study, under the most skilful teachers, of an extraordinarily adroit and subtle art. Whether, under any circumstances, oratory has quite so much practical value as we are apt to assume is beside the point; Cicero could do at will whatever can be done with it."

In the careful arrangement of his material and by his great attention to elegance of diction, as well as in variety of sentiments and

vivacity of wit, Cicero is regarded as having
excelled Demosthenes. His copiousness has
already been mentioned and has often been
criticized by ancient and by modern writers.
But his copiousness was not redundant; on
the contrary, a careful examination shows that
while Quintilian was right in saying that nothing could be added, it is equally true that nothing can be taken from his sentences without
the sacrifice either of sense or of rhythm. He
never uses meaningless synonyms, but each
word has its peculiar force and none can be
spared. He himself maintains that rhythm
must be natural and not gained by superfluous
words or an unnatural order, and he does not
fall into the error against which he warns his
readers. The younger Pliny, who was an admirer of Cicero and an emulator of his style,
as he tells us, prefers the fulness of Cicero to
the brevity of Cato and Gracchus and says of
the former's oratory: *optima fertur esse quae
maxima.*

Cicero seems to have been the first orator
to make an extensive use of wit and humor
in his speeches. In that way, and by clever
digressions, he often distracted the attention
of a jury and disguised the legal weakness of

a case. Sometimes his attacks upon his opponents were of a sort repugnant to modern taste, but he was not alone in that respect; the utmost freedom of invective seems to have been tolerated in the Roman courts and made use of in public addresses. In his *Defense of Murena,* against a charge of illegal electioneering, brought by Sulpicius and Cato, whom Murena had defeated in a consular election, Cicero obscured the issue and won an acquittal for his client by a digression, in which he declared that it was natural for the people to prefer a military man such as Murena to a jurist and a man of peace, and intimated that the times demanded a consul who was a man of action. In the *Defense of Cornelius,* as Quintilian points out, Cicero saved his client by practically admitting the charge against him, and launching into a eulogy of Pompey which had nothing to do with the point at issue. His wit served sometimes to cloud the issue but also sometimes to make his opponent or his client ridiculous.

Cicero had made a study of wit and humor as a feature of oratory as early as 55 B.C., but although he speaks of the earlier orator Crassus as famous for his wit, he found little ma-

terial of which he could make use, either in his
Roman predecessors or among the Greeks.
His conclusion is that its use is something
which cannot be taught or reduced to rules.
A recent writer has shown [30] that we have few
specimens of wit from the Athenian courts,
and that such as we have are found, not in
the speeches of the great orators, but in those
composed by the litigants themselves, and in
" the informal exchanges and proceedings per-
mitted in an Athenian court." Cicero, however, seems to regard wit as a quality which
is characteristic of Attic oratory, since he
thinks it worthy of note that none of the new
Atticists of his day make use of it. In his
opinion Lysias had a fair amount of the " Attic
salt," Demosthenes little, while Hyperides and
Demades surpassed all the rest in this respect.
Quintilian tells us that Cicero was regarded
as too fond of raising a laugh both in court
and in private, but Quintilian himself seems
to approve of Cicero's wit, for he says: *mira
quaedam in eo fuisse videtur urbanitas.*
Plutarch, on the contrary, thought that
Cicero's love of jesting led him at times into
scurrility, although that is a thing which
Cicero in his discussion of the topic declares

must be avoided. Doubtless Cicero and Plutarch would not have agreed in their definition of scurrility.

Cicero was not a little proud of his reputation for wit. He tells Atticus, with evident complacency, that Caesar is making a collection of clever sayings, and that his own are so characteristic that Caesar can reject, at hearing, a witticism attributed to Cicero which is not really his. Saintsbury, in his *History of Criticism*, congratulates us that this collection has not survived, and to judge from the specimens which have come down to us, he is right in characterizing the comic element in Cicero as of superabundant quantity and inferior quality. Certainly, many of the orator's efforts seem rather cheap when judged by modern standards, or even when compared with the wit and humor of Augustus, Juvenal, or Martial. Some of his jokes seem to aim at self-glorification; for example, the one on Rebilus, the man appointed to be consul for a single day, that he was a man of such extraordinary vigilance that during his whole consulship he did not close his eyes in sleep. This irresistibly suggests the thought that Rome once had a truly vigilant consul, who for an entire year watched over the safety and welfare of his country. Although some of Cicero's alleged witticisms, such as " Who has bound my son-in-law to a sword? " said apropos of Dollabella's short stature, appear in a slightly altered form to-day, it is not to be supposed that such modern jests are imitations of Cicero. Such obvious forms of wit are general and widespread. It is altogether probable, however, that his use of wit and humor in oratory and letter-writing has not been without its effect.

In his *Orator* Cicero gives a great amount of space to the matter of rhythmical structure, and rhythm plays an important part in his style, especially his *clausulae,* or sentence-endings, which have perhaps been excessively refined and reduced to rule by enthusiastic investigators, such as Zielinski. The importance of rhythm in Cicero's writing, however, is undeniable, and it is this feature that has often escaped the notice, not only of his superficial imitators, but even of some who have grasped and adopted the other essentials of his manner.

In the attempts to discredit Cicero, which have been general in some quarters, even his reputation as an orator has not gone unscathed. It has been maintained that he was not successful either in the senate or in the courts. But not to mention such general statements as that he " ruled in the courts," that he was a perfect orator, and the like, this allegation has been satisfactorily refuted by the investigation of an American scholar. Dr. Granrud [31] points out that in estimating Cicero's success or failure a number of factors must be taken into account. He usually appeared for the defense and not as an accuser, a circumstance which put him at a disadvantage at the outset, since the Roman courts offered less opportunity to take advantage of mere legal technicalities, of which so much is made in our own day; it was necessary to establish the guilt or innocence of the accused beyond the possibility of a doubt. Then too there was no appeal to a higher court, with its opportunities for delay and its advantage to the wealthier litigant, but a question at law was settled once for all in the court of first resort. Furthermore, the jury differed essentially from that of to-day, being composed of men of position, education and legal knowledge, some of whom were of higher rank than the pleader himself and of at least equal experience and ability.[32] Such a jury must be convinced and strongly moved in order to secure the acquittal of an accused person. It is unhappily true that the Roman juries, in spite of their high quality from the personal point of view, were not always unmoved by party or factional feeling or even superior to bribery; Cicero himself, as we have seen, was not above resorting to (or accepting) questionable means of securing his ends.

The total number of orations which Cicero delivered in court and on political questions has been variously estimated at from ninety to considerably over one hundred. Taking the lower of these figures, as one which, in his opinion, can be verified, Dr. Granrud shows that Cicero was successful in a goodly number of instances, although unfortunately it is not possible always to know the outcome of the case. He seems to have been more uniformly successful in his earlier pleas than in those of his later life, not, however, from failing powers or slighter oratorical ability, for Cicero continued to grow and to improve, but because in the latter period several counsellors spoke on the same side, and thus Cicero was only partly responsible for the result. His relative position among the orators of the time is shown by the fact that he was regularly the last speaker, thus holding the position of greatest responsibility and importance. According to Dr. Granrud's figures, seven out of eighteen speeches delivered before the people were successful, and we know of none that was certainly unsuccessful. Of forty-two in the senate sixteen were successful, while seven failed to accomplish their purpose; concerning the rest we have no certain information. In civil cases he made ten pleas, of which seven appear to have attained their end. The greatest number of his speeches were concerned with criminal cases. We know of sixty-nine such orations, in forty-four of which the orator won a verdict; he failed to do so in ten cases, and the result of the remaining fifteen is unknown. These figures, taken in connection with what we know of Cicero's general reputation from such competent judges as Seneca the Rhetorician, Quintilian, Tacitus and Fronto, are sufficient to show that he was no closet pleader and clever writer, but a successful advocate. In fact, as has already been hinted, his victory over his contemporaries was rather a hollow one; Hortensius had passed his prime, and Caesar, who was apparently Cicero's equal as an orator, had no time for court practice. Cicero generously admits Caesar's excellence as a speaker, declaring that he sees no one to whom the great Julius ought to yield the palm; that his style is " elegant as well as clear, even grand and in a sense noble." In another place Cicero remarks: " What orator would you rank above Caesar of those who have devoted themselves to nothing else? Who has cleverer or more frequent epigrams? Who is more picturesque or choice in his diction? "

Cicero's speeches have often been criticized because of their display of vanity, for the passionate hatred with which he assails his enemies, the instability of his political principles, and his apparent readiness to defend anyone and everyone. His alleged vanity and his political principles have already been discussed. As to his invective, it has already been said that Cicero was a man of strong feeling, intensely human, a good friend and a good hater. The amenities of Roman politics and of the Roman courts were not such as to oblige an orator to hold his personal feelings in check.

The most outrageous charges against personal and political morality were freely made, and Cicero's vituperation falls short of that of Mark Antony, the elder and the younger Curio, Marcus Bibulus and others, as set forth in the pages of Suetonius. As regards the last two points, we should remember that both the work of an advocate and that of a politician (using that somewhat obnoxious word in its better sense) offer peculiar conditions and temptations, to which few men either in ancient or in modern times have been able to present an undeviating and uniformly successful resistance. Not to indulge in personalities, or to draw examples from contemporary modern life, it may suffice to say that there are few lawyers to-day, at least so it seems to the layman, who would refuse to defend an individual or a corporation, if they believed the accused to be within the law, regardless of equity; or who would hesitate to secure the acquittal of a client on a legal technicality, quite unconnected with the question of abstract justice. Cicero was no more scrupulous than his modern colleagues, although he seems to have been actuated, not by the prospect of a handsome fee (which in theory was forbidden in his time), but rather by the desire of adding to his personal following and winning friends to support him in advancing his position in the state — a less sordid motive, although no higher from the standpoint of strict morality.

An advocate is the representative of his client, and his position is very different from that of a member of a jury. Having once undertaken a case, it is his duty to make it appear in as favorable a light as possible; in Cicero's own words: *summa laus eloquentiae est amplificare rem ornando*. If he is unwilling to do that, he should refuse to accept a case. He must emphasize the points which favor his client and minimize or pass by those which tell against him. He must resort to wit, to pathos, in fact to every possible means of persuading and convincing. In the *Defense of Cluentius* Cicero expresses himself quite frankly on this point, saying that anyone who expects to learn his fixed convictions from what he says in court is greatly in error. " If cases would plead themselves," he says, " no one would employ an advocate. We are engaged to give, not our personal convictions, but what the case and the circumstances demand." It has been said with good reason that Cicero would not have published his speeches in the form in which they have come down to us, if he had considered the methods to which he resorted either unfair or unbecoming.

As to political speeches and politics in general, everyone knows that politicians and even statesmen of the present day are often obliged to change their opinions to suit changed conditions. Often it is quite right and proper that they should do so, but not many are above changing their minds with an eye mainly to public opinion and political advancement or security. Cicero would have been almost more than human if, after passing through the lower grades of the " course of honors," and seeing the consulship within his reach, he had not trimmed his sails so as to take advantage of every shifting breeze. But he was always a true patriot and never sacrificed the interests of his country to his personal ambition.

The power of Cicero's oratory in his own day may be estimated from the success of his political career up to and including the consulship. He was awarded first place by those of his countrymen who were most competent to judge of such matters, and we have no satisfactory ground for questioning their verdict. The influence of Cicero on later times is undoubted, but it is more difficult to trace, for the modern technical works on oratory and eloquence are singularly silent or brief as to the historical development of the subject. His influence seems to have been particularly strong at all times in pulpit oratory, beginning with Saint Paul, Justin Martyr and Minucius Felix. The hostility of the Church to the pagan literature gradually prevailed and put a temporary end to this, but the classic influence reappeared with the rise of such great preachers as Bossuet. The indirect influence, due to the position of Greek and Latin in the education of the clergy, must have been strong, at least since the Reformation.

In political oratory Cicero's influence was first felt in England, where free debate and the institution of trial by jury offered conditions analogous to those of republican Rome. Shaftesbury, England's first great parliamentary debater, was a student of Cicero, while Chatham, Pitt, Sheridan, Fox and Burke were all indebted to Cicero and to Demosthenes. This influence is for the most part more readily felt and inferred than traced or acknowledged; but occasionally it becomes obvious. Burke specifically refers to the Verrine orations in his *Impeachment of Warren Hastings*, which in spite of the differences in the character of the accused and their degree of guilt [33] has considerable resemblance to Cicero's *Impeachment of Verres*. Burke also quotes Cicero's reply made to Hortensius, when the latter said that he could not solve enigmas: "Yet you have a sphinx in your home." The orator referred to a present made to Hortensius by the plunderer of Sicily. Boswell, as he tells us in his immortal biography, once asked Johnson if he thought that Burke had read Cicero much. To this the great lexicographer replied: "I don't believe it, Sir. Burke has great knowledge, great fluency of words, and great promptness of ideas, so that he can speak with great illustration on any subject that comes before him. He is neither like Cicero, nor like Demosthenes, nor like anyone else, but speaks as well as he can." Whether Johnson could be fair to Burke or not is a difficult question to answer; this reply, at any rate, seems to be based upon insufficient observation; for Burke's "fluency of words," as well as some of the other qualities which

Johnson ascribes to him, was acquired from study of Cicero.

With the introduction of trial by jury into France in 1790 Cicero's influence crossed the Channel. The orators of the French Revolution were Ciceronians and the expression " this was the way of the Romans " was frequent in the republican clubs. The revolutionary style of Camille Desmoulins, according to Sainte-Beuve, was spiced and, as it were, stuffed with quotations from Tacitus, Cicero and other Latin writers, which he applied to the conditions of his own time. In apologizing for them in one of the numbers of his journal Desmoulins admits " a weakness for the Greeks and Romans." There is nothing new, he declares, under the sun, and it is as well to be the echo of Homer, Cicero and Plutarch as of the clubs and cafés. He calls Cicero's *Duties* a *chef d'oeuvre* of common sense. Mirabeau founded one of his speeches on the second Catilinarian, combined with parts of the *Defense of Milo* and the *Speech for Ligarius*. A Girondin opponent assailed Robespierre in a so-called Catilinarian and was answered in a speech modeled upon Cicero's *Defense of Cornelius Sulla*. Robespierre, indeed, posed as a modern Cicero and was so called in the songs of the day. The French have always appreciated Cicero, and their eminence in oratory is doubtless due to their study of Rome's greatest exponent of the art.

Besides direct influence, so far as it can be traced, the indirect effects of the study of Cicero by future statesmen in the schools and colleges must have been at least as great. At Cambridge University in 1570 the study of Rhetoric was based upon Quintilian, Hermogenes and the speeches of Cicero; an Oxford statute of 1588 shows the use at the sister university of the same general course. In our own country Webster, Clay, Sumner and Wendell Phillips show the effects of Ciceronian studies, and we must listen with respect, if not with absolute conviction, to the words of one of America's greatest orators and most distinguished citizens, Rufus Choate. In his *Eloquence of Revolutionary Periods,* speaking of the *Philippics,* he says: "From that purer eloquence, from that nobler orator, the great trial of fire and blood through which the spirit of Rome was passing had burned and purged away all things light, all things gross: the purple robe, the superb attitude and action, the splendid commonplaces of a festal rhetoric, are all laid by; the ungraceful, occasional vanity of adulation, the elaborate speech of the abundant, happy mind at its ease all disappear; and instead, what directness, what plainness, what rapidity, what fire, what abnegation of himself, what disdain, what hate of the usurper and the usurpation, what grand, swelling sentiments, what fine raptures of liberty roll and revel there."

The comparison of Virgil with Homer for a time did much to dim the fame of the Roman poet, until it was realized that Virgil was in no sense a rival of Homer, since the *Aeneid* and the Homeric epics represent the highest development of widely different types. Equally futile is the comparison of Demosthenes and Cicero, which Quintilian ventured to make, and it has had a similar unfavorable effect upon the fame of the Roman orator. It naturally excited the jealousy of the Greeks, to whom, besides, Cicero's failings were especially odious, — in particular his levity in the courts and his vanity. As early as the third century, however, Longinus, or whoever was the author of the work *On the Sublime,* showed a larger spirit and sounder judgment. He writes:

"Demosthenes' strength is in sheer height of sublimity, that of Cicero in its diffusion. Our countryman, because he burns and ravages all in his violence, swift, strong, terrible, may be compared to a lightning flash or a thunderbolt. Cicero, like a spreading conflagration, ranges and rolls over the whole field; the fire which burns is within him, plentiful and constant, distributed at his will, now in one part, now in another, and fed with fuel in relays."

Cicero himself seems to acknowledge the supremacy of Demosthenes in the *Orator*, where he says of him: *unus eminet inter omnis in omni genere dicendi.* That is a sufficiently strong statement from a man who, as we have said, surpassed Demosthenes in some particulars; strong enough to acquit him of the charge of excessive vanity, at least so far as his eloquence is concerned. Even Demosthenes, he goes on to say, does not quite measure up to his ideal of the perfect orator, an ideal actually attained by no mortal man.

VI. CICERO AS A WRITER

IT is on his work as a writer, rather than on his ability as an advocate and orator, or as a statesman, that Cicero's fame rests most securely, and it is in this line also that his influence upon later generations of men was most marked and most salutary. Even his orations must be judged as literature; they were revised and often rewritten for publication, and doubtless contained some things which "might have been said," but were not. On the other hand, it must in fairness be admitted that they lack the impression conveyed by the speaker's effective delivery and his vivid and energetic personality. Some of the speeches, like a great part of the *Verrine Orations*, were never delivered, but were published as political pamphlets; others were elaborated and expanded for the same purpose, like the famous *Second Philippic*, to which Juvenal refers in these words:

conspicuae divina Philippica famae.

The *Defense of Milo*, as is well known, was

not at all the speech which was delivered at the trial of the slayer of Clodius, but as Cassius Dio says: " one which he wrote some time later, and at leisure, when he had recovered his courage." Dio adds: " There is also told the following story about it. When Milo in banishment made the acquaintance of the speech sent him by Cicero, he wrote back saying that it was lucky for him those words had not been spoken in that form in the court; for he would not now be eating such fine mullets in Massilia (where he was passing his exile), if any such defense had been made."

From the beginning of his career Cicero made a careful study of the art of expression, both as a speaker and as a writer. At the time when he delivered his first speeches, Latin prose, which, as in all languages, lagged behind poetry, was in a formative state. It has been said that before his time there was not a single first-class prose writer among his countrymen, and the fragments of Cato, Gaius Gracchus, and the other early orators and historians fully support such a statement. It was Cicero who raised his native tongue from the position of the leading Italic dialect to that of a world language, one which has ex-

erted a powerful influence upon all the modern
tongues of Indo-European descent. In this, as
in all the other phases of his remarkable career,
his success was due in part to native ability,
but in still greater measure to painstaking effort
and careful preparation. From his earliest
years he devoted himself to the translation
into Latin of Greek prose and verse, one of
the best possible means of learning to feel the
exact force of words and of cultivating a good
style, provided the language which is translated is one of high development and finish.
He possessed a perfect ear for rhythm, which
gave him a feeling for euphony in prose as
well as in verse, and to that feature of his
style he gave great attention. The careful
study of his orations and the comparison with
one another of those written at different periods of his life, as well as the chance com-
ments of other writers, show that he was fastidious and particular in his choice of words
to a degree which seems hardly credible. Thus
he gradually discards the form *abs*, abstains
from using *novissimus* and *novissime*, as Gell-
lius points out, although both Cato and Sallust
employed those forms, and for rhythmical effect, according to the same Gellius, used *in*

potestatem esse instead of *potestate*. If this last distinction seems too fine-spun, it might perhaps be better appreciated if Cicero were more frequently declaimed in the original Latin, with proper regard to emphasis and expression. The effect on the ear might in some instances be similar to that which, as we shall see, was exerted upon Petrarch.

Although Cicero was fastidious in his use of words, he was willing to adopt, or even to coin, new terms as occasion demanded, and particularly in his philosophical writings he was obliged to add extensively to the resources of his native tongue in order to express Greek philosophical ideas. His care and attention extended even to grammatical *minutiae*. In one of his *Letters* to Atticus he discusses the proper spelling of the word Piraeus and the question whether or not a preposition should be used in saying " to the Piraeus." He is inclined to favor the use of the preposition on the ground that the Piraeus is the name of a place and not of a town, but he appeals to Atticus for his opinion, which he says will greatly relieve his mind. He was not above resorting to evasion when a matter of usage was uncertain, for we read that when Pompey was considering the proper form of the inscription to be placed upon his theatre, and authorities disagreed as to the correctness of *tertium* or *tertio* in expressing " in his third consulship," Cicero recommended writing simply *consul tert.*, which Gellius tells us had been replaced in his day by an equally noncommittal *consul III.* Agrippa evidently had no such doubts when inscribing his name on the Pantheon; for the inscription, which is either his own or a copy of Hadrian's time, boldly reads *consul tertium*, and Gellius, who tells this story about Cicero, argues convincingly for that form.

In addition to the orations, Cicero wrote works on rhetoric, politics, and philosophy, besides a great number of letters, and made some essays in verse. In his youth he began a treatise on rhetoric, of which he completed only the part relating to the gathering of material, *De Inventione*. It was not until 55 B.C., at the age of fifty-one, that he followed this early work with one *On the Orator* (*De Oratore*), dedicated to his brother Quintus, and nearly a decade more elapsed before the *Brutus,* a work on famous speakers, and the *Orator* appeared. Although these and his lesser works on the subject are of a technical nature, they are attractive to the general reader, and are raised into the domain of pure literature, by their fine style, the interesting accounts and critiques of the principal Roman orators and some of those of Greece, and the lofty tone given them by Cicero's conviction that true oratory must be based upon philosophy and general culture and not merely upon rhetorical theory.

Of the philosophical works those devoted to politics form a class by themselves and from the nature of their subject are the most original. They represent Cicero's ideal of the proper form of government, in the form of a constitutional state like that of Rome. Of these the *Republic* (*De Re Publica*), in six books, was published before 51 B.C.; only about a third part of the work has come down to us in a fragmentary condition, and for many centuries the only surviving part was the *Dream of Scipio*, from the sixth book. Cicero's *Republic* gave rather a *résumé* of Roman legislation than a development of theory. About a year later the dialogue *On the Laws* (*De Legibus*) was begun, but apparently it was never finished; to this the work of Plato of the same title served as an incentive, rather than as a model. The rest of the philosophical works, which it is not necessary here to mention in detail, were designed to make the Romans acquainted with Greek speculative thought, in particular with the ideals leading to wise and right living. Of several of them we possess only the titles, and two of these, *On Glory* and *Hortensius,* were among his most celebrated writings.

Cicero's works in the field of rhetoric and philosophy belong to the two periods in his life when he was debarred by circumstances from active participation in politics. These were the time when the first triumvirate acquired dominant influence, and during the supremacy of Caesar. The former of these periods of enforced retirement was saddened also by the death of his beloved daughter Tullia, and in both instances he turned to philosophy as a consolation for sorrow and disappointment. The brief time in which the greater number of the philosophical works was written precluded the possibility of independent research; but Cicero showed good judgment in the selection and treatment of his topics, and he presented them in an attractive and readable form. He is over-modest — a fault with which he is seldom charged — when he says of them: *verba tantum affero, quibus abundo.* Their style has the dignity which the subject demands, but it is enlivened and given variety by the use of the dialogue form and by the introduction of frequent anecdotes. As a disciple of the New Academy, Cicero's attitude towards matters regarding which there was difference of opinion was open-minded and inquiring, and he was also receptive of new ideas and impartial in his judgment of them. Although he was not a contributor to our knowledge of philosophy, and even misunderstood and misinterpreted his sources at times, he nevertheless was successful in his attempt to arouse the interest of his countrymen in the subject, principally because of his ability to present the material in an attractive literary form. It was this feature which raised his books above the level of mediocrity, and made their influence felt both in ancient and in modern times. Many years later, when Plato's works again came to light, Cicero's adaptations inevitably suffered by comparison with their originals; but they had done a great service by keeping the study of philosophy alive before the original material was restored to us; they have also given valuable information about the works of some Greek philosophers which have not survived. In a way they fill the place in literature which in art is occupied by Roman copies of Greek masterpieces, except that Cicero's writings stand on a higher artistic level than do the greater number of such copies.

Cicero was an indefatigable letter-writer, and, as has already been intimated, he was a master of the art. In all, between eight and nine hundred of his epistles have come down to our time, in thirty-seven books, and an equal number of books are known to have been published, which have not survived. The collections which we have consist of letters written between 68 B.C. and July 6, 43, including nearly a hundred written to Cicero by various correspondents. There are sixteen books of letters to acquaintances and friends (*Epistulae ad Familiares*), including letters from some of them to Cicero, and sixteen books contain letters to Atticus (*Epistulae ad Atticum*). There are three books of letters to his brother Quintus, and two books of correspondence with Marcus Brutus. None of these letters was written for publication, but all are ordinary letters of correspondence. The letters to Atticus were probably published by their recipient, who includes no letters of his own; the others, by Cicero's favorite freedman Tiro, who also wrote a biography of his friend and patron. It is obvious that neither of these men would have published letters which they thought would damage Cicero's reputation; that they have had that effect is due in a great measure to different standards of taste and propriety in modern times, and in part perhaps to a lack of judgment on the part of Atticus and Tiro. Similar errors of judgment have not been unknown in our own day.

In his letters Cicero expresses his thoughts and feelings with the utmost freedom. As he himself expresses it: "I write in one way what I think only those to whom I am writing will read, and in another way what I think many will read." This has been done sometimes by politicians of our own day, and their revelations have returned to plague them in spite of the postscript "Burn this letter." Cicero's frank utterances have been a shock to his admirers and a joy to his detractors, but, as has already been said, his letters nevertheless furnish a model of correspondence, written in the colloquial language of educated men, the *sermo cottidianus*. They are characterized by lightness of touch, by wit and humor, and by facility and felicity of expression. The high plane on which they stood in his own day may be judged by comparing them with those of his various correspondents, including Caelius Rufus, Pompey the Great, Cato of Utica and other men of note. The contrast is even greater than that between his orations and the fragments of the earlier orators which have been preserved. Exceptions are the brief communications of Julius Caesar and the letters of Servius Sulpicius Rufus, whose beautiful letter of condolence, addressed to Cicero at the time of Tullia's death, is a model of its kind and worthy to take its place with those of Cicero himself.

The wide range of Cicero's writings, the early period of his life to which some of them belong, and the fact that in his letters he naturally unbent and used the language of everyday speech, make his vocabulary and syntax more varied and free than that of Caesar. This has led to the habit, especially in Germany, of depreciating Cicero's style in comparison with that of his great contemporary. Such criticism, however, is wholly unfair. Cicero was, as Augustus termed him, a " master of words " both in the language of literature (the *sermo urbanus*) and in that of ordinary conversation. Furthermore, he knew how to adapt his manner to the subject on which he was writing or speaking. He was, as we shall see, the standard of correct diction for future generations, while Caesar is rarely cited in that connection.

Cicero's practice in translation from the Greek included verse as well as prose. He also wrote metrical compositions of his own, which added nothing to his reputation in antiquity or in subsequent ages. He was certainly not a poet. Whether or not he thought that he was, is uncertain; but it has been suggested with reason that so much of his work in that line would not have been preserved, if he had not taken the precaution to make generous quotations from his poems in his more enduring prose works.[34] It is possible for one who is not a poet, but has a command of language and an ear for rhythm, to write poetry, or at least eminently respectable verse. An example is Lord Macaulay, whose *Lays of*

Ancient Rome have been praised or damned from that point of view by such competent judges as Mrs. Browning and Matthew Arnold, not to mention others. Cicero's poetical effusions have received scant praise and much condemnation. Tacitus satirically remarks of Caesar and Brutus, that both wrote verses, not better than Cicero, but with better fortune, since fewer men knew that they had done so. Both Quintilian and Juvenal made sport of. the luckless lines:

O fortunatam natam me consule Romam
and
Cedant arma togae, concedat laurea laudi.

Of the first Juvenal declares that if all Cicero's writings had been as bad as that, he need not have feared Antony's sword. But it is generally agreed that Cicero had a good ear, and we may be sure that he did not fail to note the jingle in the first, and the assonance in the second, of these unlucky lines. They were undoubtedly written with the intent either of attracting attention and by their very faultiness fixing themselves in the memory, or to serve as a foil to smoother and more conventional verses. Thus Ovid, we are told, sometimes mingled similar lines with his more polished verses, in the belief, as he put it, that a face is more comely in which there is some slight blemish. The lines which Seneca cites as Ovidian examples of this:

Semibovemque virum semivirumque bovem,
and
Et gelidum Borean egelidumque Notum,

are quite as eccentric as those of Cicero, and they were regarded as faulty by the friends to whom the poet submitted them for criticism, who begged him to strike them out. Cicero, it is true, lacked the divine *afflatus*, but he could write good verse and his services to the development of the dactylic hexameter seem to have been considerable.

A style of real distinction is seldom, if ever, acquired without long and painstaking effort. When the remark was made to Lord Northcliffe that " Thackeray awoke one morning and found himself famous," he replied: " Thackeray had been writing eight hours a day for fifteen years. The man who wakes up and finds himself famous hasn't been asleep." Cicero's style was no exception to the general rule. His efforts to perfect his powers of expression began early and were continued without cessation. His methods and the matters which he considered important are set forth in the *Orator,* in which he describes the ideal orator and his qualifications. In that treatise he draws a proper distinction between the oratorical and the literary or conversational styles, and he naturally gives a good deal of space to matters which concern only the spoken word, such as the modulation of the voice, the use of gestures and " action " in general, and the expression of the face and eyes. Yet a good part of his remarks are appropriate to literary style, in particular the niceties of sentence rhythm, of which he truly declares that he has said more than any previous writer on oratory.

The particular merit of Cicero's style, like that of any really good stylist, is that all this preparation and practice, this meticulous attention to the choice of words and their effective and rhythmic arrangement, are wholly concealed. There is none of the obvious striving for effect which made Augustus say of Mark Antony that he wrote rather to be admired than to be understood, and which was carried to such an extreme by some writers of

Nero's time. There is no dragging in of meaningless and superfluous words merely for euphonic effect, such as he himself criticizes in some of the Asianists and in Hegesias in particular; and there is no fantastic or unnatural word-order employed for that same purpose. *Ars est celare artem;* Cicero's consummate art, his painful and laborious training, are thoroughly and effectually hidden. His style is clear, natural, easy and unaffected, and at the same time highly finished and full of distinction. It tempts the imitator, but as Horace says of the poetry he would write:

> sibi quivis
> Speret idem, sudet multum, frustraque laboret
> Ausus idem.

In addition to those Romans who made their writing obscure by vain striving for effect, there were also those who frankly disregarded style altogether, and made no attempt to write elegantly. Such writers are obscure and hard to understand, repellant to the reader in spite of the varied and interesting contents of their works. Such a writer was Cicero's celebrated contemporary Marcus Terentius Varro, the

most learned of the Romans and a voluminous writer on a great variety of subjects. As
Cicero's fame as a statesman suffered by inevitable comparison with his brilliant contemporary Caesar, so his reputation as a scholar
was dimmed by the sound and thorough learning of Varro. Varro, however, scorned all
niceties of diction, and in the classical period
writes in the crude manner of earlier days.
Nevertheless Cicero respected and admired
him and craved recognition from the learned
man. This finally came, after Cicero had set
the example by inscribing his *Academica* to
Varro, in the form of a dedication to Cicero
of the great work *On the Latin Language* (*De
Lingua Latina*).

It is natural to inquire what constitutes the
special superiority of Cicero's style and made
him, rather than some other Latin writer, the
inspiration of the Renaissance and of the best
writers in many modern tongues. It seems
obvious that it was its clearness, simplicity and
musical quality. Sallust, Seneca and Tacitus
were good stylists, and Tacitus was far
more than that; but all three had mannerisms and peculiarities which made imitation
of them impossible, save for a few scholars

of exceptional powers; in the hands of others
the attempt resulted in caricature. Livy's
style was never successfully copied because of
his highly elaborate periodic structure and a
poetic coloring which is due to a study of the
poets and a conscious imitation of their diction and style. Cicero, on the contrary, offers
no difficulties that are apparent on the surface
and in unskilled hands the imitation of his
style appears to be more successful than that
of any of his possible rivals. Caesar alone is
equally lucid and simple, but as a model he
yields to Cicero because of the narrow range
of his surviving works and their slighter appeal to the general reader. Furthermore,
while Caesar's diction is choice and his Latin-
ity faultless, as an Atticist he lacks the musical
quality of Cicero's prose. It was this quality,
as we shall see, that attracted Petrarch before
he could understand the meaning of the words
which fell so pleasantly upon his ear; and Cicero's wide range offered models for almost
every kind of composition, including familiar
letter-writing and extending to the conversation of educated men. Even for historical
composition it was Sallust, and not Caesar,
who became the pattern of later writers.

In Cicero's hands the Latin language became an instrument of precision, capable of expressing clearly and elegantly a wide range of thought. It was without the nationalistic and unapproachable character of the classic Greek prose and free from the crudity, the unintelligibility, the mannerisms of other Latin writers. Mackail has referred to the remoteness and limited appeal of the classic Greek style; that of Sallust, Seneca, Tacitus is in the same sense nationally Roman, partaking of that cyclopean character which Skutsch happily attributed to the Latin tongue.[35] Of all the ancient Greek and Latin writers of the best periods Cicero's style is the most truly cosmopolitan, having characteristics which a good style in any language should possess; it was therefore best adapted to serve as a model for writers of other nations. In the language of Dimsdale, Cicero "fitted the Latin language to be a vehicle for philosophic thought, and achieved a style which is the basis of modern European prose."

VII. CICERO'S INFLUENCE IN ANTIQUITY

IF it should seem that a disproportionate amount of space has been devoted to Cicero's life and personality, it is in part because he still needs defense against those who belittle his achievements and malign his character; in part also because his career and his character have been in themselves a lesson to succeeding generations. It has not been the intention to give him unqualified praise, but merely to defend him against such criticism as seems excessive and undeserved. Since a great man may influence posterity either through his life or through his works, it is important to be able to form a just estimate of anyone who is in any sense a national hero. Some eminent writers offer nothing in their lives which is worthy of imitation, not infrequently much to avoid. The lives of others, on the contrary, furnish an inspiration as great as, or even greater than, their written productions. As extreme illustrations we may take Dante, the six hundredth anniversary of whose death called forth eulogies all over the civilized world, and François Villon, " the sorriest figure on the rolls of fame," as Stevenson called him. In the ancient world, perhaps unjustly, Sallust and the younger Seneca have furnished stock examples of a lack of consistency of personal conduct with ideals committed to writing. That a national hero may not be a perfect man, that his life may be marked by failures and disappointments, is shown by the career of our own General Grant, which for that very reason serves as an inspiration and an incentive. " There are few careers," says a writer in one of our daily papers, " that contain such striking ups and downs, crowned by ultimate victory over untoward circumstances. In both his virtues and his weaknesses Grant is a worthy subject for study by the young man of to-day."

Cicero was unquestionably one of the national heroes of old Rome, and his name is familiar to-day to all educated men. Therefore the thoughtful study of his life and character cannot fail to inspire or to warn in our own day, as it has done almost without interruption since he played his part in what Augustus termed the comedy of life. Since some are cast for tragic parts, Shakespeare expressed the thought better than the cynical emperor, when he said:

" *All the world's a stage,*
  And all the men and women, merely players."

If it be as true as it is trite to say that a pebble dropped in mid-ocean gives rise to wavelets which reach the remotest shores, and that a missile thrown into the air sets in motion vibrations which extend to the stars, the lives even of obscure men may exert an influence that can neither be traced nor measured. What then must be the influence of a Cicero, an outstanding figure in the last days of the Roman republic, a potent influence upon his countrymen of later times, and known to-day, at least by name, as widely as any Roman and far more widely than any save two or three? Naturally, it is the man of sufficient prominence to be remembered and recorded in history that has a lesson for future generations. In the words of Longfellow:

" *Lives of great men all remind us*
  We can make our lives sublime,
  And, departing, leave behind us
  Footprints on the sands of time."

Cicero's influence upon his own countrymen began immediately after his death. The historian Livy, in a letter to his son quoted by Quintilian, advises him to read Demosthenes and Cicero, and after them those who are most like them. As the opponent of Mark Antony Cicero's name was honored during the rule of Augustus, and at that time his son Marcus attained the consulship and became a member of the college of augurs. Cicero had the respect of the senate, since a decree of that body had named him "Father of his Country" before that proud title had become almost a conventional designation of the emperors. As Juvenal with a sting of sarcasm expresses it:

Sed Roma parentem,
Roma patrem patriae Ciceronem libera dixit.

In a similar vein the elder Pliny writes of Cicero: "I salute you, who were the first to be called Father of your Country and earned a triumph without laying aside the toga." In the schools of rhetoric, too, Cicero was a prominent figure, representing sometimes a perfect character, save for the lack of Cato's *constantia,* now serving as the target for the attacks

of budding orators. These exercised their in-
genuity in declaiming replies to the second
Philippic, searching for weak points in the Ar-
pinate's armor or inventing slanders out of
hand.

The counter-current of criticism began at
once, set in motion by that bitter cynic and
caustic critic, Asinius Pollio, who is on record
also as questioning Caesar's credibility as an
historian and charging Livy with " Patavin-
ity "; but even Pollio granted Cicero immortal
fame as an orator. Pollio's lead was followed
by his son, Asinius Gallus, who wrote a work
in which he compared Cicero with his own
father, greatly to the advantage of the latter.
The emperor Claudius, perhaps inspired by
Livy, wrote a reply to this brochure in a work
which is characterized by Suetonius as " not
without learning." As has been hinted, the
schools of rhetoric did much to blacken Cicero's character (we have an example in the
Invective, falsely attributed to Sallust), and
the Greek writer Cassius Dio is responsible,
either as author or transmitter, for a series of
calumnies whose effect has persisted through
the ages. But as at present, so in the later
Roman times, Cicero had his friends as well

as his detractors. In the age of the Antonines, Fronto calls him *summum supremumque os Romanae linguae,* in language which is unmistakable, but not easy to render into equally terse English. Fronto also refers more than once to the *Letters,* declaring that nothing in his opinion is more perfect; and in another passage he adds that all the letters ought to be read, in preference even to the orations. Quintilian, in his influential position as the first state professor of rhetoric, appointed by Vespasian, was largely instrumental in stemming the tide of criticism. He declares that Cicero is no longer the name of a man, but has become a synonym for eloquence. And in fact, his name is so used by Juvenal, Fronto, Ausonius, and at the end of the fourth century by Claudian in the line:

Carmina seu fundis seu Cicerone tonas.

There were two movements which militated against Cicero's supremacy. One was Atticism in its terse and epigrammatic form, as practiced by Sallust with Thucydides as his model; the other, an archaistic tendency. The latter also seemed to ancient critics a feature of

Sallust's writing, for that historian was said by Augustus to have garnered words from Cicero's *Origins*, while the satirist Lenaeus less politely called him " an ignorant pilferer of the language of the ancients and of Cato in particular." The archaistic movement was making its way in Nero's time, when the younger Seneca speaks of those who found Gracchus, Crassus and Curio too polished and modern, and went back to Appius and Coruncanius as their models of style. By the time of the Antonines the mode had become so general as to give the period the name of " archaistic." The elder Seneca and the best writers, few in number, in the period from Tiberius to Nero followed Cicero; but beginning with the first century of our era an attempt was made to found a rival style, which culminated in the highly rhetorical manner of Nero's reign; of this the chief exponent was the philosopher Seneca. That impulse, however, speedily waned; the writers of the Flavian epoch returned to Cicero for their inspiration and developed a style to which the name Silver Latin is most appropriately applied. Quintilian and the younger Pliny were admirers and followers of Cicero, and Tacitus

in his earliest work, the *Dialogue on Orators,*
writes in a style so similar to theirs and so
unlike that of his later writings, that the authorship of the *Dialogue* was by some ascribed
to Quintilian. In his later years Tacitus was
the latest, and by far the greatest, representative of the Silver Latin, out of which he developed an inimitable manner of his own; and
with him the Silver Latin came to an end.
Even in the late archaistic period, when Lucil-
ius was preferred to Horace, and Ennius to
Virgil, Cicero continued to be cited as a model
of correct usage by Gellius and others.

Cicero's influence was most seriously threatened by the growing vogue of the so-called
" new Latin," the *elocutio novella.* That mix-
ture of popular and archaic Latin (two things
which are often identical) found brilliant expression in Apuleius; it might have put an end
to Ciceronian Latin altogether, except for the
revival of the latter by some of the Christian
writers. The first of these from whom we have
a surviving work, Minucius Felix, follows Cicero in the form, manner of discussion and
thought of his book, a dialogue entitled *Octa-
vius,* in which the arguments for and against
Christianity are presented. In his style also
Minucius closely followed Cicero, as did Arno-

bius, and with greater success Lactantius, who won the proud title of " the Christian Cicero." Lactantius found in his model anticipations of the Christian doctrines, and he calls the third chapter of the third book of the *Republic* a well-nigh inspired utterance. Saint Ambrose, the learned bishop of Milan, was another follower of Cicero, and his *De Officiis Ministrorum,* for a long time the chief Christian manual of ethics, was practically a rendering of Cicero's *Duties* into Christian language, in which Ambrose solved the difficulties which he met by the use of allegory. He acknowledges his indebtedness to the orator at the beginning of his book in the words, *sicut Tullius ad erudiendum filium, ita ego ad vos informandos filios.* The indebtedness of Ambrose to Cicero in this work has long been recognized. An American scholar has recently drawn attention [36] to points of contact between St. Ambrose's sermon preached at the funeral of his brother Satyrus and a letter of Cicero's, written to his brother Quintus [37] during the orator's banishment.

To this imitation of Cicero by the Christian writers there were opposed, first, the growing vogue of the *elocutio novella,* which was more

familiar to the masses of the people, and, sec-
ondly, the hostility of the Church to the pagan
literature in general and, as time went on, to
some of Cicero's views in particular. The
head and front of the opposition was Tertullian, the uncompromising enemy of paganism
in all its aspects. Soon the Christian writers
were divided into two opposing camps, and
their attitudes towards the literature of pagan
Rome are expressed in the words of Tertullian
and those of the learned Platonist, Clement of
Alexandria. The former says: " Beware of
those who have devised a Stoic, a Platonic, or
a dialectical Christianity "; the latter compares the opponents of the pagan literature to
the sailors of Ulysses, foolishly stopping their
ears to the Siren music. There were some,
such as Hieronymus, or Saint Jerome, who
did not consciously imitate Cicero, but had
read him so diligently as involuntarily to
adopt his manner. After Jerome had given up
all other worldly goods, he could not bear to
part with his library, and he sinned by reading
Cicero even on fast days. He tells us that
on his way to the East he fell ill of a fever in
Syria, and his life was despaired of. He re-
flected with remorse upon the past, but found

some comfort in reading Plautus and Cicero, caring little, as he admits, for the uncouth Latin of the Psalms. In his delirium he seemed to stand before the judgment-seat and to hear the question: " What art thou? " When he replied that he was a Christian, the voice said: " No, thou art not a Christian, but a Ciceronian. Where thy treasure is, there is thy heart also." Conscience stricken, Jerome fell upon his face and took oath that he would never again possess or read books of worldly wisdom. He took up the life of a hermit, but with the best of intentions he could not at once change his style; although he avoided affectation of classicism, he showed the effect of his prolonged study of the best pagan literature. When he was taunted with this, he replied that his promise had been for the future, that it was impossible to forget entirely what he had already learned.

Saint Augustine, who so eloquently describes the charm of Virgil's writings, tells of the strong impression made upon him by reading Cicero's *Hortensius,* although it is perhaps claiming too much to say that he owed his conversion to Christianity to that source. In his *Confessions* he writes: " By the ordinary course of study I fell upon a certain book of one Cicero, whose tongue almost every man admires, though not so his heart. This book of his contains an exhortation to philosophy and 'tis called *Hortensius*. Now this book quite altered my affection, turned my prayers to thyself, O Lord, and made me have clean other purposes and desires. All my vain hopes I thenceforth slighted; and . . . I thirsted after the immortality of wisdom." [38] Cicero, however, was in accord rather with the heretic Pelagius than with Augustine and the Catholic Church, especially in believing that virtue was the result of human effort rather than of divine grace, and that each man was responsible for his own conduct, that human nature was good rather than evil, and that man's will was free. All of these views were opposed by Augustine; he was victorious in the controversy, and the Pelagians were the last of the early Christians to draw directly from Cicero, whom they exalted above Christ. But through Lactantius, Ambrose and Augustine, Cicero's ideas were transmitted to the Middle Ages.

It has been generally recognized that the Christian ethics are akin to those of the Stoic philosophy; whether we give the credit of this to Cicero, who was largely responsible for their transmission to the Church Fathers, or to Panaetius and Posidonius, from whom he derived them, does not seem after all to be a matter of much moment. It certainly is to Cicero that we owe their preservation and their influence. This relation between Stoic and Christian ethics is strikingly illustrated by the well known lines of Juvenal in which he anticipates the spirit of the prayer of Saint Chrysostom: "Shall men then pray for nothing? If you wish advice, you will leave it to the gods to grant us what is best for us and most helpful to our fortunes. Man is dearer to them than to himself." Or again, when he declares that one who meditates any crime is morally guilty of that crime.

At the beginning of the Middle Ages the influence of Cicero was still strong, for Gregory the Great (c. 540–604) wished to destroy his writings, on the ground that the charm of their style diverted young men from the reading of the Scriptures, as it had done in the days of Jerome.

VIII. THE MIDDLE AGES

DURING the Middle Ages the "new Latin" was in the ascendancy, in a more and more corrupt and debased form, and Cicero, like many other classical writers, was little read or understood. It was an age too of epitomes, which had begun to make their appearance long before, when Livy's monumental history and other great works were abridged, and now became universal. Isidore, the industrious bishop of Seville, declares that Cicero and Quintilian are too voluminous to read, and they were in fact largely supplanted by the compilations of Martianus Capella, Isidore, and others. Livy (in the abridged form) and Sallust survived as models for historical composition, and Virgil for poetry, the latter, in part at least, because of the supposed Christian spirit of his fourth *Eclogue* and sixth *Aeneid*. As an inspiration Cicero gave place to Virgil, since the tendency of medievalism was to accept authority and inculcate humility and self-repression. Dante's praise of Livy's infallibility is in the

medieval spirit, although in his *Vita Nuova*
Dante shows himself to be in advance of his
age and in individuality a forerunner of the
Renaissance. The worthlessness of earthly
wisdom was taught, and the love of glory, so
characteristic of Cicero, is one of the sins enu-
merated and punished in the *Inferno*.

As the great representative of Rhetoric, recognized as one of the " Seven Liberal Arts,"
Cicero continued to be held in some degree of
honor. His rhetorical works survived, although in an abridged and mutilated form. It
is indicative of the taste of the times that the
great triad of the *De Oratore, Brutus* and *Orator* was neglected for the *De Inventione* and
the *Topica;* the *Brutus* in fact was saved to
us only by accident and in a single manuscript.
Alcuin made the *De Inventione* the source of a
treatise on rhetoric. The great scholars of the
period were familiar with other works of Cicero and devoted some attention to them. The
Venerable Bede made a collection of his famous
sayings and is recognized as an emulator of
his eloquence in a letter of Aeneas Silvius Pic-
colomini, afterwards Pope Pius II. This letter was written to the bishop of Chichester in
1444. " It is true," he says, " that there have

been among the English some who have cultivated the eloquence of Cicero, among whom
common consent would place the admirable
Bede." Einhard, in the preface of his biography of Charles the Great, which was modeled after Suetonius' *Life of Augustus*, quotes
the *Tusculan Disputations* and shows familiarity with some of the orations. Cicero seems
to have been well known to Rabanus Maurus
and Joannes Scotus. Servatus Lupus, the
learned bishop of Ferrières, who was a notorious borrower of books, asks the archbishop of
Tours to send him a copy of Boethius' *Commentary on the Topica of Cicero*, and appeals
to Pope Benedict III for manuscripts of the *De
Oratore* and other works. Lupus thinks that
the writers of his day fall far short of the dignity of the Ciceronian style used by the earlier
Church Fathers. Also in the ninth century a
West Frank called Hadoard (Hadoardus)
made a large collection of excerpts, two-thirds
of which are from Cicero. The work is introduced by a poem, which shows that the writer
is a presbyter and a librarian in a monastery.
He expresses the hope that his book may perish sooner than fall into the wrong hands. His
excerpts begin with Tullius, *On the Nature of*

God, followed by Plato. Next comes Cicero, who, as sometimes happened in the Middle Ages, was supposed to be another person than Tullius. Then follow Macrobius, Martianus Capella, Censorinus and others. The excerpts from Tullius and Cicero show that Hadoard possessed the old corpus of philosophical works which appears to-day, more or less complete, in some of our manuscripts. It comprised the *Tusculans,* the *Nature of the Gods, On Divination,* the *Old Age* and *Friendship, Lucullus, Paradoxa Stoicorum, Hortensius, Timaeus* and *De Oratore.* That there were more works of Cicero available than were in general circulation is shown by the library catalogues. That of Cluny, for example, along with seven orations and six of the philosophical works, records two complete manuscripts of the *Epistulae ad Familiares,* and one of the *Epistulae ad Atticum,* the only mention of the latter in a medieval catalogue. The same library also possessed the *De Oratore* and the *Rhetorica ad Herennium,* which was then believed to be the work of Cicero, and the *Invectives,* which were supposed to be genuine productions of Sallust and of Cicero in reply.

In the next century Gerbert, afterwards

Pope Sylvester II, lectured on Boethius' *Commentary*. He shows special familiarity with Cicero, making frequent quotations from the orations, whose preservation is supposed to have been due largely to his interest in them. He urges a friend to take with him on a journey "the numerous speeches written in behalf of many men by the father of rhetorical eloquence." As time goes on, the knowledge of Cicero seems to increase, but the number of his works in circulation appears to be smaller. Abelard quotes only four of them. Cicero was the favorite Latin author of John of Salisbury, the most classically learned man of his time, and with Seneca, of Roger Bacon; but the former knew little of the rhetorical works, almost nothing of the orations, which he quotes only once, and of the letters only the *Ad Familiares*, although he was acquainted with a goodly number of the philosophical works. The purity of John's Latin style was doubtless due to his reading and study of Cicero. Bacon criticized the Church for neglecting the pagan literature, and thus failing to make use of the wisdom of the ancients. Dante quotes the *Duties, Old Age, Friendship,* and the *Limits of Good and Evil.* The classification of sins in Canto xi of the *Inferno* is based upon *De Officiis* i. 13, and the story of Thais as an example of flattery is taken from *De Amicitia*, 98. In the *Inferno* (iv. 141 f.) Tully is placed in the first circle, of the unbaptized, in a fair meadow at the foot of a castle, in company with Linus, " moral Seneca " and other worthies. The *Friendship* and Boethius' *De Consolatione Philosophiae* were the two works in which Dante found consolation for the death of Beatrice.

IX. THE REVIVAL OF
LEARNING

WITH the dawn of the Renaissance Cicero once more became a dominant figure; moreover, his influence was personal and not merely due to his position as one of the great classic writers of Rome. In fact, the Renaissance witnessed a rebirth of Cicero, because of the charm which his writings had for Petrarch, and this led to an awakening of interest in the entire ancient world. In addition to his attraction for Petrarch, Cicero was the natural inspiration for such a movement because of the individualistic character of his philosophy. For the Renaissance was individualistic in spirit and discarded the practice of humility and the reverence for authority which had prevailed during the Middle Ages. Petrarch, inspired by Seneca, Virgil, and in particular by Cicero, became the leader of a small group of intellectual men, who were the centre and focus of a great movement. At the period of life when other children were absorbed in fables and stories, young Petrarch, either through a natural impulse or the influence of his father, began to read and love the great Roman orator. Although at that time, as he himself tells us, he was unable to understand all, or even a great part, of what he read, he was fascinated by the music of Cicero's language; so much so that by comparison all else that he heard or read seemed dull and monotonous. As time went on, Petrarch learned to appreciate other qualities in his favorite author; he began first to imitate and then to emulate Cicero's style. While studying law at Montpellier, he continued to read Cicero and Virgil. Since his devotion to the classics interfered with the progress of his legal studies, his father undertook to burn all the volumes of Cicero which he possessed, as well as the remainder of his Latin books. He was touched, however, by his son's tears at this threatened holocaust, and accordingly rescued from the flames a Virgil and one of Cicero's rhetorical works, saying: " Take Virgil to amuse yourself from time to time and Cicero to help you study civil law."

This heroic remedy proved unavailing. As soon as Petrarch became his own master, he dropped his legal studies and began to collect

and read the works of Cicero. Indeed, it is
to him and to his indefatigable friend Poggio
Bracciolini that we owe the preservation of a
half of all the works of Cicero which we now
possess; the process of discovery was completed about fifty years after Petrarch's death.
Petrarch himself found two orations, one of
which was the *Defense of Archias,* as well as
the *Letters to Atticus* and *to Quintus,* and the
correspondence with Brutus. Poggio's discov-
eries were even more numerous, and in 1389
Cullucio Salutati found the *Epistulae ad Familiares,* which he studied so thoroughly and imitated so closely as to be the first to earn the
title of *Ciceronis simia,* "the ape of Cicero."
The *Letters to Atticus,* which were the first of
Cicero's writings to reveal his personality,
came as a rude shock to his ardent admirer Petrarch; the revelation that his idol had feet of
clay at first caused him deep distress and disappointment, but that feeling gradually gave
place to one of sympathy and increased
affection.

Cicero's letters were the first purely personal
ones produced by the ancient world, and after
his day no progress was made in the art of
familiar letter-writing until the Renaissance.

Petrarch had at first taken Seneca as his model for that kind of composition, since he was nearly forty years of age before he became acquainted with the letters of Cicero; but in his later years he preferred Cicero. The humanists in general adopted Cicero's familiar style, and as a result their letters are the most vital literary record of the period.

Not only was Cicero individualistic in his philosophy, but, when properly understood, he taught men to make their literary style the expression of their own personality. Thus Petrarch, with all his veneration for his master, did not slavishly imitate Cicero's Latin; he rather took him as a model and prided himself on the fact that his Latin style was not Cicero's but his own. But Petrarch's devotion to Cicero and his efforts to write pure Latin led to the final victory of classical over scholastic Latin, of the *auctores* over the *artes,* as the grammars of those days were called.

The effect of this movement, in which Petrarch was the leader, was two-fold. On the vitality of the Latin tongue itself, and on its use as a spoken language, the effect was disastrous; its natural development was checked and in the hands of the humanists it became for the first time a "dead language." The Latin writings of those days are, with the exception of some of the letters, mere literary curiosities. The *Africa*, Petrarch's great epic,[38a] received a crown and was regarded by its author as his greatest production; but to-day it is all but forgotten, while his fame as a poet, which among his own countrymen is second only to that of Dante, rests upon the lyrics and sonnets which he regarded as mere recreation. On the native Italian, on the contrary, the effect of Latin studies was powerful and salutary; Italian began to be cultivated as a vehicle of literary expression; or rather, the earlier impulse in that direction was given renewed strength. The movement had really begun with Dante, who at first thought of writing his immortal epic in Latin, but fortunately for his enduring fame decided in favor of the vernacular, which he had championed in a Latin essay on the common speech (*De Vulgari Eloquio*). The first master of Italian prose was Boccaccio, Petrarch's friend, like him an admirer of Cicero, and by many regarded as the greatest scholar of the age, next to Petrarch. The subjective element which enters into all literary criticism is revealed by the fact that Voigt does not rank Boccaccio high and thinks his knowledge of Cicero superficial. Even Cicero was turned into Italian at this time; Brunetto Latini translated the speeches *For Marcellus, Ligarius,* and *Deiotarus.* The impulse passed the bounds of Italy, and in 1405 De Premierfait rendered the *Old Age* and the *Friendship* into French.

The restoration of Ciceronian Latin was a slow process; the period from Petrarch to Leonardo Bruni, in the first half of the fifteenth century, was marked by a gradual purification of the language and a return to classical standards. Bruni has the credit of being the first of the neo-Latinists to write with absolute freedom from errors, followed by Guarino da Verona, Antonio Panormita, Aeneas Silvius, and others. The difficulties were enormous, since neither adequate dictionaries nor grammars were available. It was necessary besides to unlearn the barbarous Latin of the period, which was a second vernacular; it is small wonder if, with all their pains, the early humanists were unable to avoid lapses. They persevered, however, and " by the year 1500," says Orton,[39] " men could write like ancient Romans and were putting into practice the

[131]

lessons of taste, of organized reasoning and arrangement, they had slowly learnt from their models. This progress would perhaps have been a barren pedantry or a limited advance, had not the Italians themselves been undergoing a maturing change, which enabled them to perceive and acquire the intellectual wealth which the classics offered them." It was some time before the importance of rhythmical structure in the writing of Latin was realized; the first to discover it was Paolo Cortesi, who writes: "It is my opinion that the Latin language ought to be expressed in a kind of musical form, which heretofore has been wholly unknown to all the men of our time."

A pendulum well pushed is apt to swing too far, and the line which separates imitation from aping is easily crossed. Gradually " Ciceronianism " came to mean a close and slavish following of the Roman writer, and its desirability was a source of frequent and acrimonious controversy. The first to give special prominence to Cicero in this respect was Gasparini da Barzizza, who lectured on the orator at the universities and whose volume of model Latin letters of the year 1470 was the first book printed in France. He is said to

have been the first and only writer of his time
who attained a correct style, including the
proper arrangement of words at the end of
sentences. Although he is credited with being
the fountain head of absolute Ciceronianism,
he himself seems to have studied Cicero for
his spirit as well as for the mere form, and to
have made use of him as a means of imparting
general culture. Sabbadini attributes it to the
influence of Barzizza that Cicero is read, loved
and honored in the schools of Italy. His followers, however, insisted on an exact imitation
of Cicero's diction and syntax, with the rejection of all words and constructions which
were not actually to be found in the orator's extant works. This tendency was
fostered by the books which now began to
supply the lack of dictionaries and grammars,
since these were based wholly or in great
part upon Ciceronian usage. Such, for example, were the *Observationes in Marcum
Tullium Ciceronem* of Nizzolius (Mario
Nizzoli), in later editions entitled *Thesaurus
Ciceronianus*, and Scaliger's *De Causis Latinae
Linguae*, where *causis* is used in the sense of
"principles." Nizzoli's *Thesaurus* became the
vade mecum of the extremists, who refused to

tolerate any words not contained in it. Since the work was incomplete, they were not infrequently put to confusion for rejecting words which their opponents triumphantly and gleefully showed to be Ciceronian. Muretus with evident relish tells of interlarding his speech with words which Nizzoli had overlooked, and relates how his ultra-Ciceronian friends protested that such words caused them extreme torture. But when he had shown that those same words had been used by Cicero, they at once found them soft, sweet and pleasing to the ear. The tenets of the extremists were these: Latin can be acquired only by imitation; one must take some one writer as a model; the best Latin writer must be chosen; the best is Cicero.

Barzizza's view found ready acceptance in the schools, but the new movement at first met with vigorous opposition from the Church, since it was considered unchristian to imitate the pagan literature. But finally Cardinal Bembo so paganized the ecclesiastical Latin, that in the first third of the sixteenth century Rome became the very centre of Ciceronianism. A society of *litterati* actually bound its members by oath not to use any word which could not be found in Cicero. The Cardinal himself, who declared that he would rather be able to write Ciceronian Latin than be made Marquis of Mantua, was the chief representative of Ciceronianism. He refused to talk Latin except with a select few, for fear of corrupting his style. He is said to have kept forty portfolios, through which every page of Latin that he wrote passed in succession, being revised and amended before advancing from one stage of progress to the next. Into the Latin of the Church Bembo introduced such terms as *res publica* for the Church and *magistri* for its officials, besides using the Roman method of dating by Kalends, Nones and Ides. In his *History of Venice* he calls the nuns *virgines vestales*, the saints *divi*, and the cardinals *senatores*. The feeling of the time is shown by Browning's bishop, a contemporary of Bembo's, as the date " Rome, 15 — " in the title of the poem shows, who in ordering his tomb at Saint Praxid's would have in his epitaph:

" *Choice Latin, picked phrase, Tully's every word,*
  No gaudy ware like Gandolf's second line —
  Tully, my masters? Ulpian serves his turn."

Controversies on the subject of Ciceronianism began early and were carried on vigorously, and some of them have become historical. The first of these was between the celebrated Poggio Bracciolini and Lorenzo Valla, author of a work entitled *De Elegantia Latinae Linguae,* which appeared in fifty-nine editions within a hundred years and had a great deal of influence. The quarrel originated in a chance criticism of Poggio's diction by one of Valla's pupils, and it was carried on by Poggio with a wealth of invective which would have made Cicero envious. Valla showed a more temperate and judicial spirit and had decidedly the better of the argument, although his attempt to give Quintilian the place of honor occupied by Cicero was unsuccessful. Next, Politianus (Angiolo de' Ambrosini da Monte Pulciano), a great scholar, who, like some others, aimed at forming a distinctive style of his own and was fond of using uncommon words, was assailed by Scala, a pedantic Ciceronian, and by Paolo Cortesi. In the course of the discussion Politian writes: " I beseech you not to ally yourself with the superstition that nothing which is entirely your own can bring delight, that you must never take your eyes from Cicero." A third con-

troversy was that between Bembo and Gian-
francesco Pico.[40]

The most vigorous and effective opponent
of extreme Ciceronianism was the great Dutch
scholar Desiderius Erasmus, who at one time
was professor of Greek at Oxford. Erasmus
was himself a writer of elegant Latin and a
lover of Cicero. He was an opponent of Ciceronianism, so-called, not of the great Roman
himself, of whom he says in the introduction
to his edition of the *Tusculan Disputations,*
published two years before his death:
" Whether I have made progress with the advancing years I know not; but certainly I
have never loved Cicero more than I do now."
In 1528 Erasmus published a dialogue called
Ciceronianus, in which the absurdity of the
position taken by the extremists was vividly
and wittily shown. In this dialogue, which
is modeled on the *Lixiphanes* of Lucian, a Ciceronian, Nosoponus, and an anti-Ciceronian,
Bulephorus, argue the question in the presence
of a minor character called Hypologus, who
is converted to the opinion of Bulephorus. To
the tenets of the Ciceronians Erasmus opposed
tenets of his own, maintaining that Cicero
could not be imitated because his style was

individual and characterized in particular by appropriateness of expression (*aptum*); that he ought not to be imitated because the only possible result was a caricature. On the other hand, Erasmus rightly believed that Cicero's spirit could be acquired by gaining an intimate knowledge of the subject on which one was to speak or write, as Cicero himself always did, by a thorough study of rhetorical theory, and by constant practice in the reading and writing of Latin.

Another cogent argument against those who would use no word not found in Cicero is brought out by Muretus in a letter to Darius Bernardus. Having pointed out that some of Cicero's works are lost, while others exist only in a fragmentary form, he says: " If a rat or a moth had eaten a bit of a page, or mold and decay had ruined it, or a spark from the lamp had fallen on some certain part of the book, to-day the words *pigrandi* and *contraversandi* and many others would be barbarisms." The attitude of reasonable men is given expression by Sir Philip Sidney in his *Apologie for Poetrie:* " Truly," he says, " I could wish, if at least I might be so bold as to wish in a thing beyond the reach of my capacity, the diligent imitators to Tullie and Demosthenes (most worthy to be imitated) did not so much keep Nizolian Paperbookes of their figures and phrases, as by attentive translation (as it were) devoure them whole and make them wholly theirs."

Erasmus was assailed with violent invective by Julius Caesar Scaliger, in *An Oration in Defence of Cicero against Erasmus,* after some delay published at Paris in 1531. Erasmus' book also called forth a *Defence of Italy* by P. Curtius, in 1535, and numerous other controversial works, besides involving Erasmus in disputes with others who resented being mentioned in his work or felt slighted because they had been passed over unnamed. Among his quarrels was one with Budaeus (Budé), the celebrated French scholar, arising from the fact that Erasmus had mentioned him in connection with a certain Badius, a printer of no great repute. The most interesting thing about the contest is a Latin distich, in which the cause of the quarrel is immortalized:

Desine mirari quare postponat Erasmus
Budaeum Badio; plus favet ille pari.

The curricula of the schools and colleges and

the influence of the lexicons and phrase books helped to maintain Cicero's prominence. The *Thesaurus* of Stephanus (Estienne), first issued in 1532 and often reprinted, was, however, eclectic in its vocabulary and paved the way for modern lexicons and modern views, which do not undervalue Cicero and his importance, but emulate rather than imitate the great Roman.

The views of Erasmus are so reasonable and so obvious that one cannot but wonder that the slavish imitation of Cicero should have persisted in some quarters after his time, and that it has raised its head from time to time even down to the present day. It is this feeling that has relegated to comparative obscurity some Latin writers of the republic and of the empire who are looked upon as not strictly " classical," as well as the Latin writings of the Renaissance and the centuries immediately following. It is this spirit alone which can make Latin in reality a dead language. Just at present this old problem takes on a new and special interest, in view of the movement to adopt an international auxiliary language, as a means of communication, not only among scholars, as Latin was a generation or two ago, but for commercial and social intercourse as well. It would seem that, owing to natural and inevitable national jealousies, the only possible rival of Latin for this purpose is one of the numerous artificial languages, of which Esperanto and Ido are the most prominent examples. The only claim which such a language has is the alleged ease with which it may be learned; against any manufactured language may be urged its lack of traditions and of a literature, a lack which is unimportant so far as communication is concerned, but of immense moment in view of the position which an international auxiliary language is certain to have in the schools of all those countries which adopt it: there is also the instability inherent in an artificial tongue. The adoption of an artificial language would threaten the existence of Latin as a part of our educational system, since those who study but one language beside their native tongue would naturally choose the international language. This peril can be met by treating Latin in a broad spirit, recognizing its development since the days of the classical Latin writers, and the possibility, indeed the necessity, of its further growth and expansion; all this without emasculating it and reducing it to the level of an artificial tongue by arbitrary simplification and alteration. The effect of the choice of Latin as the international language would be marked and salutary, and with its permanence or extension as a part of the school curriculum would result greater refinement, broader culture and higher ideals on the part of those who carried their studies beyond the elementary knowledge required for business purposes. On the other hand, the trend towards materialism would certainly be greater, if all the studies pursued in school were made purely utilitarian in their nature and selected because of their ease of acquirement or their availability for earning a living.

The salutary effect of the revival of classical Latin upon the Italian language has already been noticed. With the spread of humanism these benefits made their way to other countries of Europe, inspiring a desire to make the vernacular in each of those lands an equally effective and cultivated form of expression. In 1551 we find the Spaniard Vives advising his countrymen to study Latin, not for its own sake alone, but in order thoroughly to purify and vitalize the mother tongue. This movement extended also to

France, as we have seen, and was fostered in Germany by Lessing and Wieland.

Not only did the form of Cicero's writings have a powerful effect upon the revival of learning, but the influence of their content was no less great. It has been said with truth that his philosophical treatises had a more far-reaching effect than any other works of the Greek and Latin writers except Plutarch's *Lives*. In the field of politics and statecraft, as the opponent of Julius Caesar and Mark Antony, he came to be regarded as the champion of republican freedom against tyranny and despotism. It is in fact to this characteristic that some of the sharpest attacks upon his fame have been due, for instance those of Mommsen, who exalted Caesar as a representative of the monarchical spirit, and slandered Cicero.

Enthusiastic admirers of Cicero trace even some of the advances which have been made in science to hints found in his writings. Copernicus in his work on *The Revolutions of the Heavenly Bodies* [41] expressly acknowledges his indebtedness to a suggestion from that source. He tells us that in his doubt about the accepted ideas of the movements of the heavenly bodies he took occasion to read all the philosophers to whom he could get access, to see whether any of them had theories which differed from those of the mathematicians at the universities of his day. " Then I found in Cicero," he writes, " that Nicetas believed the earth to be in motion. That was the impulse which set me myself to thinking about the movement of the earth." The passage to which Copernicus refers is *Academica* ii. 123, where Cicero says: " Hicetas of Syracuse thought, according to the statement of Theophrastus, that the heaven, the sun, the moon, the stars, all that is above our heads, stood still and that in the entire universe the world alone moved." It will be observed that Copernicus, doubtless quoting from memory, wrote Nicetas for Hicetas. It is true here, as it is in other instances, that Cicero is transmitting the theory from an earlier Greek source and not as his own contribution, as indeed he expressly acknowledges; but here, as elsewhere, the information would not have been available except for him.

Even more fruitful than this direct suggestion — and there were doubtless others of the same kind, for which formal acknowledgment was not given — was the general spirit of scientific doubt, questioning and experiment which informs Cicero's philosophical works. This he expresses in *De Divinatione* in the following words: " I must reply to what you have said, but in such a way as to assert nothing, but inquire into everything with a general attitude of doubt and self-distrust." Cicero indeed not only had an intense curiosity, which led eventually to criticism and experiment, to science and the Reformation; he likewise had the attitude towards authority which is the hallmark of the modern scientific and scholarly spirit. In his work *On the Nature of the Gods* he says: " Those who ask what I myself think about each matter are unnecessarily curious; for in discussions it is not so much authorities that are to be sought as the course of reason. In fact, the authority of those who profess to instruct is often a hindrance to their pupils; for they cease to use their own judgment, but accept what they know to be approved by one whom they respect." Cicero's influence in this regard is well expressed by Voltaire in the following words: " We hiss them off the stage then, those rude scholastics, who ruled over us so long: we honor Cicero, who taught us how to think."

X. THE REFORMATION

WHILE the habits of thought inspired by Cicero fostered the spirit which led to the Reformation, as we have seen, his direct contribution to that movement does not appear to have been great. Martin Luther rated him above Aristotle, in spite of the fact, as Luther says, that the Greek philosopher had more opportunity and leisure for speculation and writing, while the Roman was distracted by cares of state and other troubles. He declares that Cicero treated the finest and best of questions, the existence of God, his relation to mankind, eternal life, and related themes. His judgment of the orator may be set beside that of Augustus, with which we began our study; the German vies with the Roman in terseness and in broad-minded charity. " Cicero," he writes, " a wise and industrious man, suffered much and accomplished much. I hope our Lord God will be merciful to him and to those like him." But the austere and uncompromising Calvin, the exponent of predestination, could not bring himself to think of Cicero as admitted to heaven.

Such remarks as those of Luther were rather reflections of the Renaissance than an indication of the spirit of the Reformation, upon which in fact, so far as it was true to itself, Cicero had little direct influence. The general attitude of indifference towards him was accompanied by the open hostility of the Greeklings who began to flock into Italy in large numbers; for in order to enhance the glory of their own classic writers they belittled and caricatured Cicero. In fact, beginning with Cassius Dio, as we have seen, Greek writers and the narrow-minded among the philhellenes have been a source of defamation of Cicero even greater than the monarchists. Budaeus (Budé), who carried the revival of Hellenism into France, earned the significant title of " The Scourge of Cicero " (*Cicero-mastix*), a dubious honor which was shared by others before and after his time.

The only movement of the period of the Reformation which can be traced directly to Cicero's inspiration was, as Zielinski points out, the Italo-Polish Socianism, so called from its leaders Laelius and Festus Socinus. Poland had offered good soil for classical influences; Ciceronian Latin had made its way into that country at an early period, and as early as 1480 was declared by the humanist Andreas Brenta to be a second mother tongue. This religious movement, the basis of which was free-will and a rejection of a part of the supernatural element in Christianity, seems to have been directly inspired by the reading of Cicero. Although Cicero's influence on the Reformation was slight, yet both during that period, and of course during the counter-movement which followed, he retained a position of honor in the schools and thus his memory was kept alive. In that capacity he doubtless exerted an important indirect influence, which cannot always be traced. We have an example of it in Voltaire, of whom his examiners predicted that he would raise the standard of deism in France.

That there must have been an interest in Cicero in some quarters at this time is indicated by the fact that Nicholas Grimald, " the Judas of the Reformation," [42] made a translation of the *Duties* (*De Officiis*), which ran through ten editions in the fifty-seven years between 1553 and 1610, a degree of popularity which seems to have been attained by no other work of the time. Grimald also wrote a poem on *Marcus Tullius Ciceroes Death,* which is said to be the first production in blank verse to have been published in the English language. In 1561 John Dolman translated the *Tusculan Disputations,* and in his dedicatory epistle, addressed to "John, Bishoppe of Sarum," he mentions Grimald and intimates that he was the first to render one of Cicero's philosophical works into English. Dolman says of the *Tusculans:* "Therefore, when I had perused it over, and had founde suche profyte, and pleasure therein, as it were not possible to find the like in any Ethnicke wryter: I wyshed all men the lyke delyght, as the reading of it brought unto me."

XI. THE DEISTIC MOVEMENT

IT was the deistic movement in England in the seventeenth and eighteenth centuries which again brought Cicero into special prominence. During the intervening time his influence is not easy to trace. Montaigne, for temperamental reasons, did not rate Cicero very high. He acknowledges his eminence as an orator and praises the *Letters to Atticus*, although he understood them so imperfectly as to suppose that they were written for publication; but the philosophical works he found tiresome because of their elaboration, their prefaces, their definitions and similar features, preferring the essay method of Seneca. Of Cicero he writes: " Je ne veulx pas qu'on employe à me rendre attentif, et qu'on me crie cinquante fois ' or oyez' à la mode des heraults." But Cicero might have found consolation in the fact that Montaigne included Plato in his dislike and for the same reason. Montaigne also thought little of Cicero's verse, but he was too great a man and too just a critic to make his condemnation general. He writes:

"Neither do I know how to excuse him for thinking his poetry fit to be published. 'Tis no great imperfection to write ill verses; but it is an imperfection not to be able to judge how unworthy bad verses were of the glory of his name. For what concerns his eloquence, that is totally out of comparison and I believe will never be equalled."

Roger Ascham was a staunch Ciceronian, referring to the orator as "my master Tully, from whom commonlie I am never wont to dissent." In another passage he says: "Your owne bookes, Cicero, be as well read, and youre excellent eloquence is as well liked and loved and as trewlie followed in Englande at this day, as it is now, or ever was sence your owne tyme, in any place of Italie, either at Arpinum where ye were borne, or els at Rome, where ye were brought up." Queen Elizabeth herself studied Cicero with Ascham as her tutor; he tells us that at the age of sixteen she had read nearly all the great Roman's works, and Ascham credits her with a mastery of periodic and rhythmic prose. He himself recommends the translation and retranslation of Cicero as the best means of acquiring a good Latin style. Sir Philip Sidney's style was in-

fluenced by Cicero, although he protests
against the mere use of Ciceronian tags. He
declares that narrow Ciceronianism is the
great abuse of Oxford, where, as he expresses it, *" dum verba sectantur, res ipsas
negligunt."* Samuel Johnson was apparently
Ciceronian in his manner, but he missed two
important features of the style. Having no
ear for music, he could not appreciate or imitate Cicero's rhythmical structure. Further,
Cicero varied his long periodic sentences with
short, pithy ones, as he himself expresses it
using the poniard (*pugiunculus*) instead of
the broadsword. Johnson, as Clark remarks,
never used the dagger.

The deists denied the necessity of a divine
revelation, basing their conviction upon the
point made by Cicero in his *Nature of the
Gods,* that all men have an instinctive idea of
God and religion, and upon another tenet of
the same work, that the existence of God is
to be inferred from the orderly arrangement
of the universe. The question of Cicero's belief in God was a frequent subject of discussion by the deists, and various passages in his
works were found which seemed to them to
evince a God-fearing and inspired spirit. All

the great English writers of this period, Lord Herbert of Cherbury, Tindall, Toland, Shaftesbury, Bolingbroke, Locke and Hume, were influenced both by Cicero's style and by his subject matter. Locke in his work *On Education* recommends the study of Cicero for eloquence, of his *Letters* for an epistolary style, and of his *Duties* for morals. Hume too was a diligent student of the *Duties* and based his dialogue *On Natural Religion* upon the *Nature of the Gods,* maintaining that " the conviction of divine existence cannot be torn from the soul of man."

Voltaire, a friend of Bolingbroke, carried the latter's deistic ideas into France, thus fulfilling the prophecy which had been made by his examiners. Voltaire owed his willingness to accept this doctrine as much to his study of Cicero in the Jesuit schools as he did to his acquaintance with the English philosophers. He developed his ideas on the subject in a series of letters which he pretended were written by Memmius to Cicero. These, Voltaire said, had been discovered in the Vatican library by a Russian prince, and first translated by their finder into Russian and then by himself into French. He also tells of an imaginary embassy sent by Caesar after his conquest of Egypt to the emperor of China. The purpose of the embassy was to extend Rome's commerce and it reached its destination by way of the port of Arsinoë, the Red Sea and the Indian Ocean. During the sojourn of the ambassadors at his court the emperor made secret inquiries through his interpreters about the Roman religion and the customs of the people. He found so much that seemed to him absurd and ridiculous that he was inclined to look upon the envoys as fools or imposters. But when he learned that Caesar had set the calendar in order, and that Cicero, their greatest orator and best philosopher, had written a book *On Divination,* directed against belief in the auspices and superstition in general, he sent for the book and had it translated into Chinese, with the result that he changed his opinion of the Romans to one of admiration. Voltaire always honored Cicero and gave him repeated and complimentary mention in his writings.

Frederick the Great, Voltaire's distinguished pupil, not only became fond of Cicero in his student days, but in later life carried the *Tusculan Disputations* with him on his campaigns, as well as the *Nature of the Gods* and the *Extremes of Good and Evil*. In 1779 Frederick ordered the translation into German of the best classical writers, including Xenophon, Demosthenes, Sallust, Tacitus, Livy, and all the works of Cicero. The influence upon Prussian and German scholarship which was thus inaugurated continued to have beneficial results, until the late Emperor William II set his face against classical training and fostered and encouraged the so-called practical studies. It is a fact strangely lost sight of by the opponents of the study of Latin and Greek that the Germany of 1914 was no longer truly a classically educated country.

XII. CICERO AND THE MODERN WORLD

AS we have seen even in this necessarily brief and inadequate survey, Cicero's influence continued potent even after his death, and has endured down to our own day, varying in intensity at different periods, sometimes almost extinct and apparently exhausted, but as constantly reviving and dominating human thought. So lasting has it been, and in so many directions has it been exerted, that it is difficult to find a parallel. In the history of the early Church Cicero played an important part, purifying and elevating the style of the Christian writers and influencing their thought, warring against superstition and the belief in prodigies and magic, furnishing a code of ethics which required but slight modification to adapt it to a Christian community and to the conditions of modern life. Carried to an extreme, for those days, his belief in the power of human effort and in the freedom of man's will led to the schism of the heretic

Pelagius, which was unsuccessful in his day, but has reappeared at intervals and has partial modern analogues in Unitarianism, the Ethical Culture movement, Christian Science, and in the inner convictions of some adherents to more orthodox beliefs.

During the Middle Ages the great figure among Romans is Virgil. With him we have a return to the mystical element in religion and thought, with a corresponding rejection of human wisdom, of which Cicero was the exemplar. Thus it is Virgil who acts as Dante's guide to the Lower World, while Cicero, or Tully as he called him, finds infrequent, though honorable, mention. Even at that time Cicero's influence was not wholly lost, but like the course of one of Rome's great aqueducts, it plunged beneath the surface, to reappear with undiminished force. His rhetorical works continued to exert a strong effect upon the thought and expression of the time. His individualism, the key-note of his personality, led to the Renaissance with its tremendous influence upon the modern world and on the history of civilization. At that time his influence was all-pervasive, affecting style, language and literature, manners and conduct. If Cicero's service to the modern world had been confined to the love which he inspired in Petrarch, thereby bringing about the Revival of Learning, we could not be sufficiently grateful to him; for the effect of the Renaissance has never been wholly lost. In the words of Symonds:[43] " When we consider that before the sixteenth century had closed, they (the humanists) had imbued the whole Italian nation with their views, forming a new literature, directing every kind of mental activity, and producing a new social tone; and furthermore that Italy in the sixteenth century impressed her spirit on the rest of Europe, we have a right to hail the humanists as the schoolmasters of modern civilization."

During the period of the Reformation the influence of Calvin and the doctrine of predestination prevailed over the teachings of Cicero, and, as during the Middle Ages, the great Roman once more suffered temporary eclipse. He was not forgotten, however, since he retained his position in the schools, while his lofty character and the purity of his ethics were recognized by such a leader as Martin Luther. The deistic movement, the attempt to identify Christianity with natural religion and rationalism, once more restored him to prominence. The deists were not foes of the Church, but when their tenets were pushed to an extreme, we have a parallel to the heretical attitude of Pelagius in the position of Voltaire.

Cicero's influence has always been particularly strong in France. Montesquieu wrote: " Cicéron, selon moi, est un des plus grands esprits qui aient jamais été; l'âme toujours belle, lorsqu'elle n'était pas faible." M. de Sacy calls him the most clear and luminous of writers. Sainte-Beuve believed him to have been the only genius that the Roman people had who was equal to their empire. The English historian Gibbon read the whole of Cicero after leaving Oxford, and his style was strongly influenced by that of Cicero and Xenophon. Cardinal Newman in a letter to the Rev. John Hayes, written April 13th, 1869, says: "As to patterns for imitation, the only master of style I have ever had (which is strange considering the differences of the languages) is Cicero. I think I owe a great deal to him, and as far as I know to no one else. His great mastery of Latin is shown especially in his clearness."

In oratory Cicero's influence may be traced

from his own day through the history of the early Church, and in the pulpit oratory of various nations and periods down to our own day. With the introduction of trial by jury and of democracy his influence is extended to judicial and political oratory; in France in particular the Revolution produced a crop of speakers who owed much to his example. His influence may be felt in the best orators of subsequent times, while the principles of rhetoric are based upon his treatises on that subject. We find him figuring invariably as the inspiration to freedom and democracy and the opponent of monarchy and tyranny. His contributions in these directions are admirably summed up by Mackail, when he says: " Without Cicero the Middle Ages would not have had Augustine or Aquinas, but without him the movement which annulled the Middle Ages would have had neither Mirabeau nor Pitt."

If in this year of grace Cicero's influence is less obvious than it has been at some previous times, it is because it has been absorbed and assimilated by our modern life and forms an essential part of it, affecting our best literary style and ideals, our manners and morals, in fact our entire civilization. He has been happily compared to a lens, which focuses and transmits to us the scattered rays of his time.[44] If his direct influence does not lie upon the surface of events, it is even more difficult to trace the strong current set in motion by the study of his works in the schools, almost, if not quite, without a break, from his own day to ours. We find a remarkable record of the influence of Roman writers on men of eminence in various walks of life in such books as the *Value of the Classics*, published by Princeton University in 1917, and in other books of the kind. But as Horace says:

> Vixere fortes ante Agamemnona
> Multi; sed omnes inlacrimabiles
> Urgentur ignotique longa
> Nocte, carent quia vate sacro.

So too the effect of the study of Cicero on less prominent but perhaps equally useful citizens is buried in oblivion, because they have found no essayist to make known their reactions and achievements. One example of the kind has been given us in Miss Martha Baker Dunn's essay, *Cicero in Maine*. " I believe," she writes, " as I look back now, that our first conscious inspiration towards what was best in literature and noblest in statesmanship took root from that time." She tells how her teacher, in answer to a question from one of the class, " gave us a brief sketch of the great Roman's life, showing us how his true nobleness overbalanced his political weakness and vanity. He, the teacher, ' knew a man ' who had visited Tusculum and seen the spot where the ruins of Cicero's villa still stand, with the great ivy tree growing against the sunny wall, and he made it all the more real by reminding us that this was the same Tusculum with those long ' white streets ' we were so familiar with in Macaulay's poem." Later in life " the uncouth lad," as she calls one of her schoolfellows who afterwards achieved success, expressed himself as follows: " My own first conscious impulse towards making a good citizen of myself dates from the time when I was awkwardly but enthusiastically translating Cicero's orations in the old brick schoolhouse in my native town." That too is an influence which any man might be proud to have exerted. If it is widespread — and who can measure it — it is no less glorious, no less helpful to mankind, than to have inspired a Renaissance. If this were a pedagogical essay, it would be in place to point out that whether Cicero is to the schoolboy an inspiration to good citizenship and lofty endeavor, or a conceited old word-monger, depends largely upon the teacher under whose guidance he is studied.

Has Cicero really a message for this twentieth century and for a people so self-sufficient as our own, living under conditions apparently so different from those of his day? Has he a lesson for the " hundred per cent American " ? We have the answer to this question in his own words: " Not to know what took place before one's birth is to be always a child. For what does the lifetime of man amount to, unless it be combined with the record of past history and the ages of men of old? " As in the field of scientific investigation, the scholar does not begin *de novo,* but builds upon the results obtained by his predecessors, just so in politics and statesmanship, and in all the departments of life, the experience of the past should guide us or warn us. To our country above all the history of republics, past and present, and in particular that of the great Roman republic, its successes, its failures and its final downfall, should have a peculiar value.

In the last days of that republic, as we have seen, Cicero was a dominant figure, although he was not successful in stemming the tide that swept the state from freedom into ultimate despotism.

To the individual, as well as to the state, the life of Cicero may teach more than one lesson, and the thoughtful study of his career, under sympathetic and competent guidance, offers abundant inspiration to the young men and young women who read his works at an impressionable period of their lives. His earnestness of purpose in our somewhat frivolous age, his thorough and careful preparation for his life work in these days of haste and short cuts, his lofty idealism when there are so many temptations to materialism, all these may well be taken to heart. From him too we may learn love and respect for our native tongue and the desire to use it, both in speaking and in writing, as effectively and elegantly as possible. That this lesson is one particularly needed by our young people of school and college age is shown by the fact that anything approaching elegance of diction, which of course is a thing quite apart from affected language or " fine writing," is regarded as pedantic and the mark of the " high-brow," which is worse than the mark of the beast. At an age when the students of foreign countries — so far as the writer's observation goes — pride themselves upon their mastery of their native languages and in differentiating their speech from that of the vulgar, our young folks, apparently from a kind of linguistic self-consciousness and a desire to avoid the extreme reproach of being " high-brows," restrict their vocabulary and cramp their powers of expression by the free use of slang gathered from the vaudeville stage and similar sources. During the period of education one should cultivate the use of one's mother tongue, and the methods followed by Cicero in his effort to speak *pure et Latine* are still effective, *mutatis mutandis;* for the reasons which he gives for practicing translation from the Greek apply to-day to translation from either Greek or Latin, and warn us not to attempt to learn English by the study of English alone. " In taking the writers of Latin as a model," he writes, " I found this difficulty, that Ennius, if I busied myself with his verses, or Gracchus, if I took up one of his speeches, had already used the words most appropriate to the subject. If I used the same words that they did, it profited me nothing; if I used different language, it was positively harmful to me, since I accustomed myself to use less appropriate terms. Therefore I decided, and I formed the habit in my youth, to study the speeches of the greatest Greek orators. After reading these, I turned them into Latin, thus using the best words, but yet those in common use, and also coining some words that were unknown to our countrymen, provided they were suitable to my purpose."

Cicero may give inspiration also to those who desire to perfect themselves in the valuable accomplishment of public speaking, and in letter-writing of the better sort, which is rapidly becoming a lost art in these busy days. Those who have left school or college for the university or for extra-academic training for life may find inspiration in Cicero's individualism, his independence of authority, his belief in personal responsibility as the result of freedom of the will. Patriotism is one of the greatest of virtues, when tempered with the broader international spirit and the feeling of the brotherhood of man which modern conditions counsel. In Cicero's day the nations were

comparatively isolated; to-day rapid transit
and the means of easy and speedy communication have brought them nearer together,
economic conditions have made them depend-
ent one upon the other. Still, love of country,
when it does not degenerate into chauvinism
and national selfishness, is the mark that dis-
tinguishes the good citizen from the bad, and
this quality Cicero possessed to an unusual
degree and put on record. From Cicero too
one may learn a true religious spirit, fully in
accord with the enlightened liberalism of the
present day. He did not, of course, believe
in the gods and goddesses of the Graeco-
Roman mythology. To him, as afterwards to
Augustus, religion was a powerful means of
unifying the state. He therefore believed in
the good effect of the general observance of
the ancient rites and ceremonies handed down
from early Roman times. As he himself expresses it: " Our ancestors were never wiser
or better inspired by the gods than when they
decided that the same persons should preside
over religion and the government of the republic. By this means magistrates and priests
unite to save the state." He was truly religious in spirit, with a profound belief in a
supreme being, ruler of the universe.

Finally, Cicero offers an example of one who possessed to an eminent degree the moral virtues of honesty, chastity and temperance in an age when those virtues were not common in the men whose names appear on the pages of history. In this regard he forms a striking contrast with Caesar, Octavian, Antony and some other prominent men of his time.

Such is human frailty that there are few men whose lives do not offer warnings as well as inspiration. Without undue censoriousness, or general and extravagant condemnation, we may be led by Cicero's career to shun vanity and self-praise, to aim at greater firmness of purpose without obstinacy or unwillingness to change one's mind when it is right and proper so to do, and to avoid the other minor faults and blemishes which rob a noble character of perfection. Cicero has drawn for us the picture of a perfect orator, such a one as never existed, and in all probability could not exist; in the same way we may set before our eyes the model of a perfect man, and for those who strive to create such a model Cicero offers much in the way of inspiration. Even his death and the failure of his hopes for the restoration of liberty may teach the valuable lesson that the vanquished is sometimes the victor, and that it is better to have failed in a noble effort than to have won a shameful triumph. Velleius Paterculus, writing in the reign of Tiberius, says in substance: "You accomplished nothing, Mark Antony, in causing the death of Cicero. You took from him an anxious life, old age, and an existence which under your rule would have been worse than death; but his fame and the glory of his words and deeds you rather increased than took from him. He lives, and will live, in the memory of all ages. Future generations of men will admire what he wrote against you, and execrate you for what you did to him."

NOTES AND BIBLIOGRAPHY

NOTES

1. Cassius Dio, XLVII. 9. This story seems to be accepted by A. C. Clark and others.

2. Suetonius, *Augustus*, 79. 1.

3. For March 26, 1922.

4. Suetonius, *Augustus*, 86.

5. *Greatness and Decline of Rome*, New York, 1909; III, p. 189.

6. The term "new man" (*novus homo*) was applied to one who was the first of his family to attain one of the curule offices of aedile, praetor or consul, and thus become a member of the nobility.

7. *Inst. Orat.*, XI. 1. 17 ff.

8. *Curiosities of Literature*, New York, 1881; I, p. 126.

9. *Essays*, New York, 1862; III, p. 340.

10. *Kultur der Gegenwart*, Berlin and Leipzig, 1905; I, viii, p. 332.

11. Petersen, p. 454.*

12. Sallust, *Jugurtha*, 35. 10.

13. X. 77 ff.

14. The *De Petitione Consulatus*. Quintus Cicero's authorship of this book has been disputed, but is now generally accepted.

15. Sallust, *Jugurtha*, 64.

16. J. Martha in *Mélanges Boissier*, Paris, 1903, p. 365.

17. I, p. 453.

18. See in particular E. Norden, *Die antike Kunstprosa*, Leipzig, 1898.

19. The *lex Villia annalis* of 180 and Sulla's legislation of 81 B.C. determined the minimum age at which the va-

---

* References by the name of the writer only are to works mentioned in the bibliography.

rious magistracies should be held and the intervals which must elapse between them. After the time of Sulla thirty-one seems to have been the minimum age for the quaestor-ship, forty for the praetorship and forty-three for the consulship.

20. For a sympathetic account of the life of the younger Cicero see F. F. Abbott, " *The Career of a Roman Student,*" in *Society and Politics in Ancient Rome,* New York, 1909, pp. 191 ff.

21. The holding of the aedileship between the quaestor-ship and the praetorship was voluntary. Since the aediles had charge of the public games, the office gave a good opportunity for winning the favor of the people. Caesar's games surpassed all previous entertainments in their magnificence and added to his load of debt. On the other hand, Mamercus, as Cicero tells us, lost the consulship by omitting the aedileship and its obligations.

22. This decree, in the words " let the consuls see to it that the commonwealth suffer no harm," was almost equivalent to a proclamation of martial law; but see Petersen, pp. 237 ff. The legal and constitutional justi-fication of Cicero's execution of the conspirators has been much discussed; it receives strong support from the reso-lution which Clodius caused to be passed by the senate on Dec. 6, 57 B.C., that Cicero had forged the decree of the senate ordering the execution.

23. The Sempronian law provided that their provinces should be assigned to the consuls by lot, before the election.

24. This title was conferred by his soldiers upon a victorious general by acclamation, and confirmed by the senate. After the word became a title of the Roman emperors, it was retained with its original signification, and it might be conferred several times upon an emperor, because of victories in the field.

25. This last point is questioned by Hooper, p. 91.

26. *De Bello Civili (Pharsalia),* I. 130 ff. The trans-lation is that of Nicholas Rowe, London, 1720, and often reprinted.

27. The jurors for any particular trial were selected by lot from a panel of four hundred and fifty eminent citizens, entered each year in an *album* by the praetors in charge of the courts. At times this panel consisted solely of senators, at other times of equites. In Cicero's time it was made up of senators, equites and a lower order, called *tribuni aerarii*, probably representing the commons.

28. Augustus declared (Suet., *Aug.*, 101. 3) that during the last twenty years of his life he had received in legacies from his friends 1,400,000,000 sesterces, or about $70,000,000.

29. This was a special commission appointed by a Julian law to divide Campanian lands among the commons. Membership on the commission would have assured Cicero of Caesar's favor.

30. R. J. Bonner, "Wit and Humor in Athenian Courts," in *Classical Philology*, XVII. 97–103 (1922).

31. See Bibliography.

32. See Note 27.

33. See Canter (in *Bibliography*) and A. Edward Newton, *A Magnificent Farce*, Boston, 1921.

34. A. S. Pease, Cicero *De Divinatione*, University of Illinois, 1920, p. 100.

35. Fr. Leo, *Kultur der Gegenwart*, Berlin and Leipzig, 1905; I, viii, p. 415.

36. R. J. Deferrari, "St. Ambrose and Cicero," in *Philological Quarterly*, I. 142 (1922).

37. *Ad Quintum Fratrem*, I. 3. 3.

38. *Confessions*, III. 4. Translation by W. Watts, in *The Loeb Classical Library*, New York, 1919. For Cicero's influence on Petrarch's *Africa* see Mustard, *American Journal of Philology*, XLII. 97–121 (1921). [D. M. R.]

39. C. W. Previté Orton, *Outlines of Medieval History*, Cambridge, England, 1916.

40. For a full account of these controversies, with much of the original literature in translation, see Scott's *Imitation of Cicero*.

41. *De Revolutionibus Orbium Caelestium,* Basileae, 1540; cf. dedicatory epistle to Paulus III, Pontifex Maximus, p. iv.

42. See L. R. Merrill, in *Publications of the Modern Language Association of America,* XXXVII. 216 (1922).

43. J. A. Symonds, *The Renaissance in Italy,* Vol. II. The Revival of Learning, New York, 1888, p. 536.

44. G. Showerman, "On the Teaching of Cicero," in *The Classical Journal,* III. 261–270 (1908). Cf. Duruy, *History of Rome,* Mahaffy's edition, London, 1883 ff.; III, p. 457.

BIBLIOGRAPHY

ABBOTT, FRANK FROST, *A History and Description of Roman Political Institutions*. Boston, 1911.[3]

BOISSIER, G., *Cicéron et ses amis*. Paris, 1905.[13]

CANTER, H. V., "The Impeachments of Verres and Hastings: Cicero and Burke," in *The Classical Journal*, IX. 199–211 (1914).

CHOATE, RUFUS, *The Eloquence of Revolutionary Periods*, in his *Works*. Boston, 1862.

CLARK, A. C., "Ciceronianism," in G. S. Gordon, *English Literature and the Classics*. Oxford, 1912.

DUNN, MARTHA BAKER, *Cicero in Maine*. Boston, 1905.

FORSYTH, W., *Life of Cicero*. London, 1864.

FOWLER, W. WARDE, *Social Life in Rome in the Age of Cicero*. London, 1909.

GRANRUD, J. E., "Was Cicero Successful in the Art Oratorical?" in *The Classical Journal*, VIII. 234–243 (1913).

GREENIDGE, A. H., *The Legal Procedure of Cicero's Time*. Oxford, 1901.

HOOPER, W. D., "Cicero's Religious Beliefs," in *The Classical Journal*, XIII. 88–95 (1917).

KELSEY, F. W., "Cicero as a Wit," in *The Classical Journal*, III. 3–10 (1907).

MACKAIL, J. W., *Latin Literature*. New York, 1904.

MIDDLETON, C., *A History of the Life of Cicero*, London, 1741.

PETERSEN, T., *Cicero*. Berkeley, Cal., 1920.

SANDYS, J. E., *Harvard Lectures on the Revival of Learning*. Cambridge, England, 1905.

SABBADINI, R., *Storia del Ciceronianismo*. Torino, 1885.

SCHANZ, M., *Geschichte der Römischen Litteratur*. Munich, 1909.[3]

BIBLIOGRAPHY

SCOTT, IZORA, *Controversies over the Imitation of Cicero.* New York, 1910.

SHOWERMAN, G., "Cicero the Stylist," in *The Classical Journal,* VIII. 180–192 (1913).

SIHLER, E. G., *Cicero of Arpinum.* New Haven and London, 1914.

STRACHAN-DAVIDSON, L., *Cicero and the Fall of the Roman Republic.* New York and London, 1894.

TAYLOR, H., *Cicero.* Chicago, 1916.

TROLLOPE, A., *Life of Cicero.* London, 1880.

TYRRELL, R. Y., and PURSER, L., *The Correspondence of M. Tullius Cicero.* Dublin and London, 1879 ff; I,[2] 1885.

VOIGT, G., *Die Wiederbelebung des klassischen Altertums.* Berlin, 1893.[3]

WENDELL, BARRETT, *Traditions of European Literature, From Homer to Dante.* New York, 1920.

ZIELINSKI, TH., *Cicero im Wandel der Jahrhunderte.* Leipzig and Berlin, 1912.[3]

Our Debt to Greece and Rome

AUTHORS AND TITLES

AUTHORS AND TITLES